Black Women in Reality Television Docusoaps

Rochelle Brock and Richard Greggory Johnson III
Executive Editors

Vol. 45

The Black Studies and Critical Thinking series
is part of the Peter Lang Education list.
Every volume is peer reviewed and meets
the highest quality standards for content and production.

PETER LANG
New York • Bern • Frankfurt • Berlin
Brussels • Vienna • Oxford • Warsaw

Adria Y. Goldman & Damion Waymer

Black Women in Reality Television Docusoaps

A New Form of Representation or Depictions as Usual?

PETER LANG
New York • Bern • Frankfurt • Berlin
Brussels • Vienna • Oxford • Warsaw

Library of Congress Cataloging-in-Publication Data
Goldman, Adria Y.
Black women in reality television docusoaps: a new form of representation or depictions as usual? /
Adria Y. Goldman, Damion Waymer.
pages cm. — (Black studies and critical thinking)
Includes bibliographical references.
1. African American women on television. 2. Reality television programs—United States.
I. Waymer, Damion. II. Title.
PN1992.8.A34G65   791.4508'996073—dc23   2015003544
ISBN 978-1-4331-2778-6 (hardcover)
ISBN 978-1-4331-2777-9 (paperback)
ISBN 978-1-4539-1568-4 (e-book)
ISSN 1947-5985

Bibliographic information published by **Die Deutsche Nationalbibliothek**.
Die Deutsche Nationalbibliothek lists this publication in the "Deutsche
Nationalbibliografie"; detailed bibliographic data are available
on the Internet at http://dnb.d-nb.de/.

© 2015 Peter Lang Publishing, Inc., New York
29 Broadway, 18th floor, New York, NY 10006
www.peterlang.com

All rights reserved.
Reprint or reproduction, even partially, in all forms such as microfilm,
xerography, microfiche, microcard, and offset strictly prohibited.

TABLE OF CONTENTS

	Introduction	1
Chapter 1.	Black Women's Mediated Depictions: An Overview	27
Chapter 2.	Docu-Soaping Black Women	37
Chapter 3.	Does Majority or Minority Cast Status Matter?	53
Chapter 4.	Reclaiming Sexuality	63
Chapter 5.	Black Motherhood	71
Chapter 6.	Physical Appearance	79
Chapter 7.	She Has Her Own (Money)	87
Chapter 8.	Girl Fight	97
Chapter 9.	Who Is She Repping?	105
Chapter 10.	Why Are Viewers Calling for Boycotts?	111
	Conclusion	119
	References	129

INTRODUCTION

The origins of reality TV can be traced to the 1940s launch of *Queen for a Day*, an early US game show. Since its emergence, the genre of reality television has grown in presence and popularity among producers and consumers. We might assume that these unscripted, yet heavily edited, shows present reality to their audiences. However, scholars have found that many audience members acknowledge and accept the fact that reality television is not real (Andrejevic & Colby, 2006; Biressi & Nunn, 2005; Clissold, 2004; Gillan, 2004; Gray, 2009; Stern, 2005). Many producers and directors acknowledge the extensive participant recruiting and editing processes that go into the production of reality television shows (Andrejevic, 2004; Ouellette & Murray, 2009; Pozner, 2010). Thus, one could argue that the reality in these television shows is actually a *constructed reality*—produced by the editors, rather than the actual participants. So what does this *constructed reality* say about Black women in contemporary US society? We begin this exploration, first, by assessing what others have written about women's roles, in general, in reality television. Then we discuss what reality television is, its effects, and potential implications of mediated depictions of women in these programs. We can then establish the basis for this project and begin to interrogate Black women's depictions in reality television in general and in docusoaps, a subgenre of reality television, specifically via #EnoughisEnough.

Women in Reality Television

Reality television has helped to increase the number of female representations in media (Gauntlett, 2008). However, history proves that increased representation does not always result in more accurate representations or quality representations. Pozner (2010) examined the appearance of women across several different subgenres of reality television. She argued that "reality television has emerged as America's most vivid example of pop cultural backlash against women's rights and social progress" (p. 240). Scholars such as Pozner argue that producers are opposed to women's liberation and use stereotypical and demeaning images to keep women down; however, the blame for such images is too often placed on female participants who sign up for the shows and female viewers who continuously tune in and watch such representations. The editing process and strategically altered contexts frame female participants in a particular way. Participants are "molded into predetermined stock characters" that fit certain stereotypes (Pozner, 2010, p. 28). These constructed images deliver messages on how these women are supposed to behave. In addition, these images teach women what they should regard as the key to their happiness and success. Pozner maintains that these images are especially damaging to the millions of women who are avid viewers of reality programming.

A major theme that emerged from Pozner's analysis is that female participants' physical appearance is extremely important in reality programming, as has historically been the case for most female television roles. However, reality television magnifies this ideology. In reality television women's physical appearance is communicated as being the key to success in the workplace and in romantic relationships (Pozner, 2010). Although this point of view is pervasive in reality television, a certain physical appearance is not the only imperative that these shows deliver to and about women.

Pozner also argued that women in reality television are governed by one (or more) of four traditional stereotypes:

1) that "women are catty, bitchy, manipulative, and not to be trusted—especially by other women" (p. 98). Pozner explained that women learn that their one true enemy is other women. This damages the

female solidarity that has gained women so much success in modern society. This female versus female mentality is reinforced particularly through countless girl-on-girl physical and verbal fights;
2) that women lack intelligence and common sense. Pozner explained, "Reality producers may have cut their teeth on 'dumb blond,' but they want viewers to believe female stupidity knows no racial limits" (p. 110). Educated women with successful careers are rarely cast;
3) that "women are incompetent at work and at home" (p. 117). The second and third stereotypes are often tied to traditional gender norms, as women are expected to limit themselves to domestic roles. Countless reality programs show women depending on their more intelligent working husbands. Their inability to handle domestic duties is marked as a failure;
4) that "women are gold diggers" who are after men's money and the luxurious lifestyles they can provide (p. 127). Pozner argued that this communicates the idea that "every woman has a price" (p. 130). In addition to finding someone to support them, reality television teaches women that they all need to find a husband. A single female is not presented in a favorable light. The older the single woman is, the worse single life is made to seem. Women on reality television are shown as finding the pursuit of love more important than education and careers.

During their search for "Mr. Right," female participants are often portrayed as being extremely emotional and hypersexualized. Yet, as much as the hypersexualized character is featured, she is also condemned for behaving in this manner. Her male counterparts, on the other hand, are allowed to behave the same way and yet they receive praise. Pozner's discussion offers a general overview of the problems with female portrayals in reality television. It is important, however, to highlight other research on women's portrayals in specific subgenres of reality television. We discuss research on women's portrayals in popular subgenres of reality television: competition shows, lifestyle shows, makeover shows, and dating shows.

Women in Competition Shows

Competition shows are those in which participants compete for some large prize (usually money). Typically, the prize awarded to the winner is large enough so that the contestant would not normally be able obtain the equivalent amount quickly via traditional means such as work. Participants can compete individually, as a pair, or in a group. Edwards (2004) stated that, "one of the clearest explorations of gender role stereotypes occurs in the subgenre of competition game shows" (p. 227). Within these shows, Edwards found that traditional gender roles and stereotypes were reinforced rather than challenged. Women were framed as being less physically fit than male contestants. Because the majority of competitions were based on physical strength, Edwards asserted this presented women as inferior competitors. If a female was a strong competitor in such activities, she was considered an exception; thus, women were framed as weaker and inferior to men.

Waggoner (2004) also found that women were presented in more objectifying ways than men. An examination of *Survivor* revealed that the competition show focused on the females' sexuality and physical appearance. The show communicated the idea that a woman's most valuable attribute was her appearance. Waggoner wrote, "Female sexuality [was] constructed as a potentially valuable survival tool for certain women on the show" (p. 218). Moreover, "…those women whose bodies do not fit the standard represented by these images (i.e., large breasts, flat stomachs, and firm buttocks) [were] eliminated early in the game" (p. 219). Cameras focused on females' bodies in limited clothing, thereby presenting them as "products for fetishization" (p. 219). Ironically, women who used their sexuality to advance throughout the competition were punished. Women were supposed to use their sexuality only as a "commodified object of heterosexual desire [that] has value only for those who consume it" (p. 219). These studies demonstrated that portrayals of women in competition shows reinforced traditional gendered norms and stereotypes.

Women in Lifestyle Shows

Lifestyle reality shows feature individuals taking part in certain traditional activities such as raising children, running a household, or getting married. Stephens (2004) examined the images and messages in two lifestyle shows—*The Baby Story* and *The Wedding Story*. Both shows on the TLC network followed heterosexual couples having a baby or getting married, respectively. The analysis revealed that dominant ideologies were communicated about marriage and parenting. Both shows communicated the idea that marriage and children were necessities for affluent, heterosexual couples. Although Stephens did not demarcate specific images of women, these two institutions (parenting and marriage) typically constitute the primary roles that women are traditionally bound to in and by society.

Relatedly, Fairclough (2004) analyzed *Wife Swap*, a reality show that features two families that switch wives/mothers for a specific amount of time. Viewers watch as families have to adjust to new family members, living arrangements, and rules. Fairclough argued that the images in this program were troubling as they reinforced dominant ideologies about domesticity. Within the lifestyle shows, "…women [were] either portrayed as commodities, desperate individuals obsessed with marriage," or in *Wife Swap's* case specifically, women were "entirely measured by their success in the domestic sphere" (p. 344). The show reinforced the ideology that women were expected to stay within their domestic roles. If a woman's career was mentioned, it was framed as having a detrimental effect on the household (because the household should have been the woman's primary responsibility—not her job).

Additionally, in *Wife Swap* women were presented as having unpleasant, fault-finding personalities, especially when they were shown criticizing other women for their domestic skills or lack thereof. Men, on the other hand, were presented as the calm spouses who had nothing bad to say about others. In rare instances, the show did shine a light on domineering husbands and the oppression such men inflicted upon their wives. However, Fairclough argued that, overall, the show only presented women in restrictive, non-flattering ways.

Engstrom (2009) examined another marriage-oriented lifestyle show: *Bridezillas*. Findings showed that the program reinforced the ideologies surrounding traditional marriage. Men were usually absent, and women were more invested in planning the wedding. Unlike Stephens' (2004) findings, Engstrom found that on *Bridezillas*, women of any social and financial status could be a bride. At first glance, this appears to be an empowering trait for women, but a deeper look at the program revealed otherwise. Engstrom asserted, "While the bridezillas in this program might at first appear as decisive, confident, and in control, the subsequent images of them calling other women 'bitch', losing their tempers over minute details, and generally behaving badly…uncovers that mask" (p. 11). Not only were the female images not empowering overall, the program reinforced the stereotype that women were bitches. According to Engstrom, common ideologies about gender differences were reinforced in *Bridezillas*. Men were never shown having emotional or hysterical outbursts about the wedding, unlike the women. This reinforced the idea that men are calmer and more "in control" than women (p. 11).

These three studies all demonstrated that portrayals of women in the lifestyle show subgenre reinforced gendered norms and stereotypes.

Women in Makeover Shows

Makeover programs feature individuals who undergo different treatments and procedures to alter their physical appearance. Banet-Weiser and Portwood-Stacer (2006) argued that all makeover programs reinforce the widely held belief that "looks" are important for happiness. Such shows mostly feature women who are attempting to "attain a cultural ideal of feminine attractiveness…" (p. 268). Ideal femininity is presented as a goal that can be obtained through "making better purchases, adopting better lifestyle habits, and undergoing cosmetic surgery" (p. 269). This ideal beauty can be achieved by changing the features of women who are not considered traditionally attractive.

Banet-Weiser and Portwood-Stacer found that, unlike beauty pageants, the makeover shows they analyzed demystified ideal beauty. The shows illustrated how the perfect female body can often be created rather than being a result of genetics. This presentation reinforced the notion that this created ideal beauty was necessary in order for women to be truly happy even though such ideal beauty was far from natural. In short, not meeting the criteria for ideal beauty was no longer an excuse because women had the means to purchase this beauty that society considers a necessary commodity. The pressures, pains, and financial burdens attached to attaining this ideal femininity were not mentioned. The focus of the show was to present the women who eventually became beautiful through the recommended procedures. An interesting yet relevant aside is that non-White women are often featured on these makeover shows in order to "fix" their ethnic features in order to adhere to Eurocentric beauty standards (Pozner, 2010). These findings show how physical appearance is still communicated as important and how makeover shows reinforced gendered norms and stereotypes.

Women in Dating Shows

The dating program is one of the subgenres of reality television that has garnered the most research attention. These shows present male or female participants who are all competing for the affection of one dater. Gray (2009) researched the presentations of women across several different programs and highlighted the extremely edited nature of dating shows. He also added that, "many critics worry about the patriarchal messages and reinforcement being offered to audiences" (Gray, 2009). Audience members tune in to dating shows to view both the actual dates and the reactions of the daters. Gray found that unruly women were often featured on dating shows. Their behavior was considered likeable if it was also accompanied by humor.

Women's physical appearance was also a major focus within these programs. Men were often heard commenting on females' body parts and whether those women/body parts met with their approval. The female participants' constant criticizing of other cast members' appearance helped communicate the need for beauty in these competitions. Gray also found that dating shows "reward[ed] women for relishing the roles of sexual object and spectacle and of the old duality of [M]adonna or whore" (p. 266). Female participants were often shown performing tasks that highlighted their sexuality in order to win the male dater's affection. Reality television's tendency to present women as both critical of others and focused on appearance resurfaces in this subgenre.

In his analysis, Gray discussed the potential of reality dating shows. First, he argued that women were able to exercise power when they were featured as the dater selecting the winning male. Gray also found that the occasional humor in dating shows works to challenge gender expectations. For example, the recurring image of the unruly woman could be read as females acting in opposition to the "expected and traditional dating behavior" (p. 275). Gray concluded that these images will be read as more restrictive or more empowering depending on the audience members. Female viewers' identification with female cast members will determine how critical they are about the presentations.

Graham-Bertolini (2004) focused on the presentations of women in *Joe Millionaire*. His analysis revealed that ideologies and traditional notions of patriarchy were reinforced by the show. Graham-Bertolini found that "*Joe Millionaire* glamorize[d] traditional notions of appropriate demeanors for women, and normalize[d] ideas about roles acceptable for women to assume and the goals women should aspire to" (p. 341). With the help of editing and staged events, women's main goal was presented as the search for love. This quest for romance was framed as being more important than their careers. Women were labeled as marriage material if they were domestic, pure, and submissive. Women were also rewarded if they willingly complied with "conservative societal expectations" (p. 343). Graham-Bertolini argued that editing combined with a focus on romance foreshadows women's powerlessness.

Johnston (2006) researched the similarities between reality television and 18th-century fiction. Within her analysis, she focused on *The Bachelor*, which, she maintained communicated a "monolithic version of femininity" (p. 122). Women were framed as either the good girl or the bad girl: "The 'good' girl was defined in contrast to her other, the 'bad' girl, who gamed, flirted shamelessly, and 'painted'. Often the bad girl was 'bad' because she has turned her back on domesticity" (p. 122). 'Painted' refers to the heavy make-up that the bad girl wears in contrast to the natural beauty that the good girl possesses. The good girl also wore less revealing clothing and was considered more lady-like. Again, this harkens back to the Madonna/whore dichotomy. Furthermore, the good girl was dedicated to finding true love; a male's financial standing did not affect her feelings for him. Women who were focused on men's financial assets were considered bad girls. Those women would also fit into Pozner's (2010) trope that women in reality television are gold diggers. Johnston found that the show did feature educated women with successful careers. However, these women were also presented as being willing to give everything up for love. This only reinforced the idea that women were more occupied with the quest for love. Their focus on romance at the expense of education and careers is yet another common theme that emerged.

Dubrofsky (2011) also examined images of women in *The Bachelor*. Dubrofsky found that the show reinforced "a mainstream standard of beauty; invit[ed] the male gaze; [illustrated women's] willingness to compete with other women for a man; priviledg[ed] finding a husband and having a family overall all else" (p. 123). Women who did not meet the required beauty standard were not even cast for the show. The women who did qualify as physically attractive had to agree to sexual objectification. Dubrofsky argued that female participants had to demonstrate certain qualities traditionally linked to women. For the most part, female participants were expected to be highly emotional. Dubrofsky (2009) referred to the emotional scenes featuring women as "the money shot" for reality television. The focus on women as emotional sexual objects is consistent across other reality television subgenres.

Ironically, Dubrofsky (2011) argued that *The Bachelor* promises female empowerment. Dubrofsky highlighted how producers assert that the decisions women make in the show are their own choices, not the producers'. This freedom to compete for love and decide how to present themselves is labeled as an empowering option for women. Dubrofsky, however, argued that this is not a true source of empowerment for female participants. Let us now turn to discussing what reality television is, its effects, and the potential implications of its mediated depictions of women.

Reality Television Programming

Although the reality within these programs may be artificial, the potential effect of these messages is real. Viewers often expect television content to be a reflection of reality, regardless of the genre (Croteau & Hoynes, 2003; Danesi, 2008; Meyers, 1999). Thus, even if reality television images are purely fictional, these carefully created and edited messages may still communicate ideologies that can influence audience members' actions and beliefs. Research shows that all media messages play a role in shaping audiences' views, attitudes, behaviors, and perceptions of people and issues (Abraham, 2003; Holtzman, 2000; Linn, 2003; Mazzarella & Pecora, 1999; Walsh-Childers, 2003). We will now define reality television and discuss its scope and influence in society.

What Is Reality Television?

Researchers define reality television as a form of factual programming that functions to entertain huge audiences and garner large profits (Biressi & Nunn, 2005; Corner, 2009). Audience members have begun to expect this type of programming, while cable and broadcast networks consider it crucial in their line-ups (Ouellette & Murray, 2009). Audience expectations are so intense "that it is difficult to imagine television without [reality television]" (p. 7). These expectations also hint to the staying power of this programming and its label as "the norm" (Holmes & Jermyn, 2004; Madger, 2009).

Different production practices and the use of non-actors are two of the key elements that distinguish reality television from scripted programming (Biressi & Nunn; 2005; Madger, 2009). Reality television's content is expected to "capture life as it happens" (Clissold, 2004, p. 49). In order to do so, reality television relies heavily on the surveillance of non-actors. "Ordinary people" agree to have their lives and experiences serve as the shows' main source of content (Andrejevic, 2004; Dubrofsky, 2011; Johnston, 2006, p. 119). This unscripted material combined with cast testimonials is presented to audiences in a narrative structure (Andrejevic, 2004; Biressi & Nunn, 2005; Corner, 2009; Dubrofsky, 2011).

A major misconception of reality television and its many subgenres is that it is a fairly new type of programming (Andrejevic, 2004; Dunkley, 2002; Holmes & Jermyn, 2004; Ouellette & Hay, 2008). In actuality, reality television has been in existence for decades. Researchers differ as to what they consider to be the first reality show and the date when the genre was created. One reason for this confusion is that various definitions of reality television exist. Therefore, in order to trace reality television back to its origins, the genre first must be defined.

Defining Reality Television

The hybrid nature of reality television is one of the major reasons why it is so difficult to define (Holmes & Jermyn, 2004; Murray, 2009). These shows combine different elements that are borrowed from other types of programming. For example, researchers have identified several elements of documentary and soap operas within reality television (Andrejevic, 2004; Murray, 2009; Pullen, 2004). There has also been a link identified between reality television and psychology. The shows are sometimes viewed as social experiments since they record individuals reacting to certain situations (Biressi & Nunn, 2005; Pozner, 2010). The hybrid production style of reality television "…erodes the boundaries between a variety of standard formats as well as the formal conventions that helped distinguish between them" (Andrejevic, 2004, p. 71). In addition, Holmes found that the combination of different elements also "blurs the lines between fictional and factual forms of programming" (Holmes, 2004, p. 114). Its hybrid nature and lack of boundaries make it difficult to define reality television.

Another reason why reality television is difficult to define is because the hybrid nature of the genre makes it impossible to use a general definition that includes all subgenres. A definition that is too basic includes any type of programming that incorporates reality in some way, such as news, game shows, and sports (Andrejevic, 2004; Friedman, 2002; Holmes & Jermyn, 2004). Specific and complex definitions of reality television can help set boundaries. Thus, a narrow definition is necessary before starting to research the genre.

Several scholars have defined reality television in various ways (Andrejevic, 2004; Biressi & Nunn, 2005; Dubrofsky, 2011; Holmes & Jermyn, 2004; Ouellette & Murray, 2009; Raphael, 2009). Oftentimes, the specific definitions of reality television share a few elements, such as the use of non-actors, narrative structure, and unedited material. However, several distinguishing factors determine what shows are considered reality programming. Kilborn (1994) defined reality television as:

> ...recording 'on the wing', and frequently with the help of lightweight video equipment, of events [through means of voluntary surveillance of and] in the lives of individuals and groups; the attempt to simulate such real-life events through various formats of dramatized reconstruction; the incorporation of this material in suitably edited form into an attractively packaged television programme [in narrative form] which can be promoted on the strength of its reality credentials. (p. 423)

We choose to adopt Kilborn's (2004) definition because this definition captures several elements of reality programming. For example, the definition discusses the use of "real-life events" experienced by individuals and groups. By not specifying the need to use ordinary people, Kilborn's definition can also include reality programs featuring celebrities in their everyday lives. The definition also acknowledges the importance of editing: Although the material is unscripted, Kilborn explains how the material is re-packaged. A few additional elements were added (see, specifically, what was added in the brackets in the quote above) to Kilborn's definition in order to create further boundaries for what can be considered reality television. Voluntary surveillance is an important source of the genre's content. The current definition emphasizes the need for *voluntary* surveillance. This excludes all non-fiction programming that relies on hidden cameras for their unscripted material. Although participants agree to have their footage used *after* it is recorded, this definition requires voluntary submission to surveillance before recording begins. The current definition also states that reality programming is presented in a narrative structure for the purpose of entertainment. This added element draws from several other definitions of reality television which all stress these two features (Andrejevic, 2004; Biressi & Nunn, 2005; Corner, 2009; Dubrofsky, 2011; Holmes & Jermyn, 2004; Ouellette & Murray, 2009; Raphael, 2009). Based on this definition, we ask the key question—how "real" is reality television?

How Real Is Reality Television?

Reality shows promise authentic material, but the pursuit of profit often outweighs the pursuit of realism. Hence, most critics and viewers agree that reality television is not real despite the name of the genre (Andrejevic, 2004; Clissold, 2004; Dubrofsky, 2009; Holmes & Jermyn, 2004; Johnston, 2006; Pozner, 2010). Production teams employ several different strategies to construct their desired messages. Although footage is unscripted, it is edited and crafted into what producers consider to be entertaining messages (Andrejevic, 2004; Biressi & Nunn, 2005; Dubrofsky & Hardy, 2008; Pozner, 2010). When participants do not give editors enough material to craft a profitable narrative, producers often change the context of the show. Creating different situations for the participants to deal with creates more potential footage for the show's storyline (Andrejevic, 2004).

The casting process behind reality television is also strategic. Talent scouts cast individuals who have the appearance and personality necessary for a show's plot. During casting calls, individuals who can deliver drama, sex appeal, and other money-making qualities are hired. Participants are also chosen based on their perceived ability to attract outside media attention (Banet-Weiser & Portwood-Stacer, 2006; Gillan, 2004; Ouellette & Murray, 2009; Pozner, 2010). After individuals are cast, their actions are monitored in the editing room. Critics argue that participants do not have the opportunity to represent themselves on screen, because editors decide what the audiences will eventually see (Palmer, 2002; Pullen, 2004). Viewers must also realize that the presence of cameras and production teams can also influence the way individuals behave and interact (Biressi & Nunn, 2005; Couldry, 2009).

The presence of cameras, strategic casting, and editing all contribute to the constructed reality of reality television. Researchers have argued that it is important for audience members to recognize these programs as constructed (Gillan, 2004; Holmes & Jermyn, 2004; Ouellette & Murray, 2009). Several scholars have found that although viewers understand reality television presents a constructed reality (Andrejevic & Colby, 2006; Biressi & Nunn, 2005; Clissold, 2004; Gillan, 2004; Gray, 2009; Stern, 2005), some audience members still believe these programs deliver some level of realism (Andrejevic & Colby, 2006; Clissold, 2004; Stern, 2005). Viewers are drawn to shows that can appear to be realistic despite their constructed nature. Characters that viewers identify with are considered authentic (Biressi & Nunn, 2005; Gillian, 2004). Shows are enjoyable if they can deliver a well-constructed, "entertaining, and convincing picture of reality" (Biressi & Nunn, 2005, p. 3).

Even with a constructed reality, reality television maintains its appeal. As mentioned earlier, it offers producers a cheap and profitable type of programming. Advertisers are continuously attracted to the genre because it gives them the ability to promote their products within the shows' content. But, what is less obvious is the appeal that constructed reality shows present to their viewers and participants.

Reality Television's Appeal to "Ordinary" People

Individuals are eager to participate in reality television, despite their knowledge of the strategic editing processes behind these shows. Participants are normally not compensated for their appearance unless they win monetary prizes in competition reality shows or have some celebrity status. Some participants who make a name for themselves on the show do receive money for appearances and endorsements once the show has aired. If a person is a huge success on the show, thereby helping to earn ratings, he or she may also use this new status to negotiate payment for a subsequent appearance. However, this income is not guaranteed and is not the sole motivation for participating (Andrejevic, 2004).

Some people consider participating in reality shows to be a therapeutic learning experience. Appearing on the show and interacting in different situations allows individuals to learn about themselves (Andrejevic, 2004). Some people also enjoy the opportunity to appear in reality television shows because it gives them a position normally reserved for celebrities. Furthermore, it gives participants the feeling that they are sharing the power with production teams. That is, their ability to provide material gives them the perceived power to take part in a process that is normally restricted to members of the television industry (Andrejevic, 2004; Biressi & Nunn, 2005; Ouellette & Murray, 2009)

Viewers of reality television are also attracted to the power-sharing that the genre allows. Andrejevic (2004) explained how reality television shows often create websites that allow viewers to participate in the show by providing feedback and suggestions. In addition, audiences are attracted to reality television because it is less predictable than scripted programming. Although they accept the fact reality programming is constructed, they find it less contrived than genres such as sitcoms and dramas. Reality television provides them with an exciting alternative. The non-actors who are used in reality television are considered to be more like ordinary people and, thus, relatable. Not only are they able to relate to non-celebrities, but they realize they have the same opportunity to appear on a show (Andrejevic, 2004; Ouellette & Hardy, 2008; Pozner, 2010; Pullen, 2004). Boylorn (2008) explained how this identification can even take place if audience members do not agree with all of a participant's actions.

Viewers also enjoy reality television because it provides a "fly-on-the-wall perspective" (Murray, 2009, p. 65). Audience members feel like they are in the room with participants as they watch the story unfold on their television screens. The genre can also have a voyeuristic and emotional appeal for its audiences. Some viewers enjoy tuning in for the narrative's suspense and humor (Andrejevic, 2004; Ouellette & Hardy, 2008). Aside from entertainment, the shows are also appealing because of the advice that they provide about how to handle certain situations (Ouellette & Hardy, 2008). There are instances when audience members disagree with the extreme messages communicated but continue to tune in (Boylorn, 2008; Pozner, 2010).

The appeal and staying power of reality television make the genre research worthy. Producers, advertisers, and audiences acknowledge these programs' constructed reality. However, research shows that even fictional or scripted programming can affect its audiences. Researchers are beginning to examine the power of reality television. Distinctions have also been made between the genre's *potential* power and the power it now exercises. Understanding the power of the genre helps explain why it is important to examine reality television images of women in general and images of Black women specifically.

Potential of Reality Television

Critics argue that the potential of reality television is quite promising. If the genre functions in a certain way, several positive effects could arise. According to Fairclough (2004), life-changing messages could be communicated through reality television. Pozner (2010) argued that "reality television has the potential to tell compelling stories in ways that enlighten audiences, subvert conversion, and defy expectations… (p. 265). This enlightenment comes largely from the diversity that reality television could provide. The genre opens up the opportunity for more diverse casts to appear on television (Andrejevic, 2004; Andrejevic & Colby, 2006; Ouellette & Murray, 2009; Pozner, 2010; Pullen, 2004). Groups that are normally silenced may have a better chance of being included in reality television programming. However, the debate continues on how reality television handles this diversity. The investigation of Black women's roles in reality television in this book contributes to this debate and discussion.

Reality television also has democratic potential for its audiences and participants. Its interactive nature causes viewers to feel that they are taking part in the production process. Participants of the shows feel that they are sharing power with production teams because of their contribution to the shows' content. Giving audiences and participants a voice in the production process has the potential to create a unique, democratic television genre. As key players on the show, silenced groups could find a platform to speak, which would help to empower audience members as well as show participants (Andrejevic, 2004; Biressi & Nunn, 2005; Holmes, 2004; Ouellette & Murray, 2009). However, many argue this potential is often overshadowed by reality television's power to erode society through negative imagery.

Questioning the Power of Reality Television

Another debate surrounding reality television is whether the shows have any social or cultural relevance. Although some people support the potential of reality television, others question if "…the genre evidences our society's moral decay" (Johnston, 2006, p. 115). It has been argued that reality television lacks the quality necessary to promote positive change (Jermyn, 2004). Relatedly, Pozner (2010) found that some show creators and producers feel that their shows do not have any social relevance, arguing that the shows are created to simply entertain their audiences. Even if entertainment is the sole motivation of creators and producers, these shows have the same cultural power and influence as other television genres (Ouellette & Hay, 2008).

Regarding the influence of reality television, oftentimes audience members consider the information in reality programming to be educational. Johnston (2006) argued that audience members sometimes would prefer to believe information from constructed reality over their own lived reality. Pozner's (2010) interviews with reality television viewers revealed that storylines can be so engaging that oftentimes the fictional aspect of the show is forgotten. At this point, the information communicated is absorbed as valuable, realistic information. In sum, reality television can and does educate audiences about social issues, different phenomena, people, and how to handle various situations in everyday life (Andrejevic, 2004; Biressi & Nunn, 2005; Kraszewski, 2009; Ouellette & Hay, 2008; Pozner, 2010).

One way that reality television educates audiences is through the reenforcement of common ideologies. Researchers have found different reality television shows have reinforced widely held societal beliefs about different groups, just like other genres of television (Andrejevic & Colby, 2006; Banet-Weiser & Portwood-Stacer, 2006; Bell-Jordan, 2008; Engstrom, 2009; Johnston, 2006; Kraszewski, 2009; Ouellette & Murray, 2009; Palmer, 2002; Pozner, 2010; Pullen, 2004; Stephens, 2004). Communicating such ideologies reiterates that the dominant views are the correct way of thinking

(Couldry, 2009). Reality television also communicates stereotypes about specific groups, just like other mass media (Cavender et al., 1999; Dubrofsky & Hardy, 2008; Pullen, 2004). These ideologies and stereotypes, combined with the editing, shape the way viewers interpret the programs' messages. It is important to acknowledge the fact that reality television entertains an active audience just like other media (Gray, 2009). Boylorn (2008) stated, "the danger [of reality television images] is embedded in the inability of some consumers to distinguish between reality and fiction on the television screen" (p. 421). The ideologies, stereotypes, and frames communicated through reality television still have a strong effect on its active audience members.

Evaluating Reality Television

Many critics argue that the genre has failed to meet its potential and only manages to abuse its power. The term "reality television" is sometimes used interchangeably with "trash television" (Schroeder, 2006). Some critics feel it is guilty of "dumbing down" programming with its images and messages (Biressi & Nunn, 2005, p. 24; Holmes, 2004; Schroeder, 2006). The argument has been made that reality television has failed to democratize television, as it promised. Instead, participants of shows are exploited as cheap labor. The way they are edited and the consequences of those portrayals are of no concern to production teams. These critics argue that it appears that profit is more important than sharing concerns with audiences and viewers (Andrejevic, 2004; Holmes, 2004; Johnston, 2006).

The promise of diversity is another area where reality television is said to have failed. When diversity is included, it is often driven by profit rather than a desire for social change. For example, Bell-Jordan (2008) argued that "reality [television's] impulse to 'air' racial issues has often been inspired by ratings and driven by multinational conglomerates looking for ways to captivate and titillate their audience" (p. 368). The goal is profit and not social change. Although the genre has also been found to present *and* confront stereotypes, these shows are in the minority (Pullen, 2004). The majority of shows have been credited with reinforcing stereotypes of groups rather than making challenges (Banet-Weiser & Portwood-Stacer, 2006; Pozner, 2010).

Although these observations and arguments are important, Schroeder (2006) explained how "reality television has had little meaningful analytical attention…" (p. 180). Opinions of reality television are noteworthy, but additional research is necessary to truly assess the problem. Studies focused on women's roles in reality television are few but increasing. Additionally, no study to date has focused on the presentation of Black women in docusoaps. However, the exploration of how Black women are depicted in docusoaps is central to this book.

Defining a Docusoap

A docusoap features a reoccurring cast and presents their day-to-day routines in a narrative structure (Bruzzi, 2000; Biressi & Nunn, 2005; Murray, 2009). This subgenre of reality television is most closely related to observational documentaries (Biressi & Nunn, 2005; Bruzzi, 2000). These shows "…tend to focus on the everyday lives of their subjects in somewhat 'natural' settings without a game setup, use cinéma vérité techniques, and do not contain flagrantly commercial elements such as product placement or the promise of prizes" (Murray, 2009, p. 67). Biressi and Nunn (2005) defined the subgenre as "…multi-part series, each episode featuring strong recurrent 'characters' engaged in everyday activities, whose stories are interwoven in soap opera style" (p. 64). Due in part to this format, researchers have found the docusoap to be one of the most powerful subgenres of reality television (Biressi & Nunn, 2005).

Given the influence of docusoaps and the power associated with their form, we ponder: How are Black women depicted in docusoaps? Do the depictions align with past trends that have portrayed Black women in a negative light? Or are the depictions of Black women in docusoaps more flattering and contrary to those trends, especially considering the potential, reach, and power of reality television? Research on docusoaps can help determine how Black women are presented there and can further contribute to discussions on the societal import of presentations of Black women in the media.

Why Examine Black Women in Docusoaps?

Examining Black women in docusoaps is warranted because issues of women's representation in media predate reality television and the docusoap. Scholars have examined different mediated ideologies about women and the way in which those ideologies can influence perceptions of women (Byerly, 2007; Caputi, 1995; Cramer & Creedon, 2007; Croteau & Hoynes, 2003; Douglas, 2004, 1994; Gauntlett, 2008; Macdonald, 1995; Meyers, 1999; Rogers, 2003;

Rowe, 1995). Historically, women have been featured less than men in media, especially in television. On television, the women were often featured in co-starring roles that reflected gender stereotypes and were presented as being dependent on the male characters (Croteau & Hoynes, 2003; Holtzman, 2004; Meyers, 1999). Scholars argued that both the women's rights movement and feminism can be credited for increases in women's media inclusion. Each movement illuminated unfair treatment of women in media (Croteau & Hoynes, 2003; Meyers, 1999).

These movements' successes, however, mostly benefited White women; moreover, such success did not completely remove the stereotypical images of women presented or eliminate their underrepresentation. In sum, all women have suffered from media exclusion and sexist messages; however, non-White women have also historically been treated as "the raced other" (Byerly, 2007, p. 224) and were most often the subject of racist media messages as well (Croteau & Hoynes, 2003; Wilson, Guiterrez, & Chao, 2003). More specifically, Black women have historically been portrayed as stereotypical characters that are demeaning. These images date back to the antebellum era in the US and have traveled through time via mediated messaging—with the most common stereotypes being the Mammy, Sapphire, and Jezebel (Collins, 1998; Hudson, 1998; Speight, Thomas, & Witherspoon, 2004; West, 1995). Black women's media representation has increased over the years, but researchers argue that stereotypical images still persist (Croteau & Hoynes, 2003; Entman & Rojecki, 2000). Relatedly, scholars have begun to discuss how images of women in reality television reflect, not challenge, past ideologies (Douglas, 2010; Pozner, 2010).

This finding that reality television reflects earlier ideologies is alarming, given the power, pervasiveness, and reach of reality television (Banet-Weiser & Portwood-Stacer, 2006; Engstrom, 2009; Kraszewski, 2009; Palmer, 2002; Stephens, 2004). More important, this finding is troubling because reality television has the ability to frame people and key societal issues (Couldry, 2009). One such framing and issue of import is in the area of race. Due to the ability to tell and frame a story over extended periods with recurring casts, reality television in general and the docusoap specifically could be powerful media in which to discuss issues of race in meaningful ways; however, these media have failed to live up to that ideal.

For example, Bell-Jordan (2008) examined the role race played in three reality television shows—*Black.White*, *The Real World-Denver*, and *Survivor–Cook Islands*. Each of the shows featured race in its storylines, but none succeeded in trying to improve race relations or facilitating dialogue about racial issues. Instead, the programs only framed the issue of race as an individual problem that did not require group action. Racial conflict was shown, but the issues were left unresolved. Thus, viewers were not given an example of how to handle their own racial conflicts. Some cast members were also featured attempting to dispel myths and stereotypes, which is clearly a positive step in reality television. However, as Bell-Jordan (2008) explained, the shows never problematized race nor discussed the implication of the racial stereotypes that were the root of much of the racial conflicts on the shows. These findings show that each program failed to promote diversity, inclusion, and dialogue in meaningful ways. In a similar vein, Kraszewski (2009) examined the role race played in *The Real World* and also found that the complexity of racism was not communicated. The production team used "casting, filming practices, editing, and narrative strategies" to guarantee race was discussed within the show (p. 208). Participants of different racial backgrounds were shown interacting and addressing conflict. However, the show did not succeed in communicating the severity of race issues in society. Both of these studies illustrate the strategic presence of race in reality television. Furthermore, each study demonstrated how the shows failed to use the platform of reality television and the diversity of their casts as a means to become key contributors to discussions of race relations in society.

Despite these few efforts to use reality television and docusoaps in ways that are of societal benefit in general and portray positive images of Black people, Pozner (2010) argued that negative media portrayal of Blacks, especially Black women, has continued in reality television. Moreover, researchers find that that the ideologies produced about all women—especially Black women—in reality television are problematic and oppressive (Pozner, 2010). In a similar vein, Boylorn (2008) examined representations of Black women in reality television and concluded that common stereotypes depicted most of the women as "voluptuous, loud, brown-skinned with weave down their backs and wide eyes made for rolling, fake nails and an attitude for days" (p. 419). Moreover, she found that Black women could increase their camera time if their behavior was especially outrageous. Ultimately, Boylorn concluded that these images of Black women are especially damaging because they are expected to represent "real Blackness" (p. 421).

This depiction of "real Blackness" is problematic, especially when "real Blackness" is diametrically pitted against Whiteness; in fact, reality television more times than not privileges Whiteness (Dubrofsky, 2011). Andrejevic and Colby (2006) argued that Black women are cast as the other, in comparison to White cast members; thus, Whiteness was considered to be the norm, while Blackness was considered abnormal, the aberration. In a similar vein, Dubrofsky's analysis of *The Bachelor* revealed that, "...women of color exist[ed] but were mostly irrelevant to the dominant narrative, except to the extent that their actions work to frame the white star's journey to finding his ideal mate" (p. 33). Non-White women were featured in *The Bachelor* only in order to display White women as the perfect catch and evaluate the behaviors of White cast members. Once these duties were fulfilled, these few Black women were eliminated. Although Whiteness being privileged in reality television negatively affects Black characters and the images they represent to society, many argue that the most damaging effects result from the overly negative depictions of Black women. In fact, Pozner (2010) argued that "long-term exposure to tropes about women as stupid, incompetent, gold-digging bitches may begin to affect the way adults see themselves, their relationships to friends, loved ones, and coworkers, and their own place in public and private life" (p. 131). Tyree (2011) examined images of Black men and women in three subgenres of reality television—game docs, talent contests, and docusoaps. Tyree argued that the most common three stereotypes of Black women were the angry Black woman, the hoochie (also known as the gold digger and the pigeon, see Stephens and Phillips, 2003), and the chicken head. The angry Black woman is reminiscent of the bitch character discussed by Collins (2005). These characters are usually uneducated, possess little social status and use sex as their primary commodity.

This discussion of negative media representations of Black women is not happening exclusively in the academic literature. In fact, members of the popular press (Barnes-Thomas, 2010; Reid, 2011; Viera, 2011; Zook, 2010) have argued that the images of Black women in the docusoaps are most troubling and have potential damaging effects on impressionable audiences. According to several bloggers and journalists, these restrictive, stereotypical roles in docusoaps are especially harsh for Black women (Barnes-Thomas, 2010; Reid, 2011; Viera, 2011; Zook, 2010). The popular press also explained how these images of Black women can be problematic. Viera (2011) wrote, "It is only inevitable with multiple reality shows portraying Black women as jezebels, mammies, sapphires and tragic mulattos, audiences will walk away believing this to be true representations of Black women. And those images transfer into how Black women are viewed and treated in their everyday lives" (para 6). Similarly, Samuels (2011) stated:

> From Oxygen's *Bad Girls* to Bravo's *Real Housewives* franchise, the small screen is awash with [B]lack females who roll their eyes, bob their heads, snap their fingers, talk trash, and otherwise reinforce the ugly stereotype of the 'angry [B]lack woman.' (para 3)

Reid (2011) echoed these thoughts in arguing that the image of the angry Black woman appears at an alarming rate. Reid argued that this constant portrayal of Black women as angry and aggressive negatively impacts Black female viewers, who often choose to mimic these behaviors. Some reality actors, however, disagree. In an interview, Kandi Burruss—reality star, recording artist, and songwriter—defended the stereotypical presentations of Black people in reality television. She said,

> Before I even joined the show everybody was talking about how it brought down the image of [B]lack people and [B]lack women. But I always tell people when you come on a reality show you're not trying to represent for a whole race, you're just doing you (Bitchie & Kimmy, 2011, para 2).

Despite Burruss's and other reality television stars' opinions, research shows how media images are often used by viewers as a source of information about different groups—even more than their first hand experience (Elliot, 2003). Thus, the media representations of a few Black women can be and often are used to evaluate real-life Black women.

Bloggers are not alone in expressing their displeasure with Black women's depictions in docusoaps; Black actresses have also voiced their disappointment in reality television portrayals and the negative stereotypes communicated. Actress and reality television star, Holly Robinson Peete, acknowledged that reality television presents all groups in stereotypical ways. Her issue is with the imbalance of such images for Black women compared to other groups. Peete explained, "Listen, there are plenty of [W]hite women acting a fool on television every night....But there's a balance for them. They have shows on the major networks—not just cable and not just reality shows—about them running companies, being great mothers, and having loving relationships. We don't have enough of that" (Samuels, 2011, para 5).

More seasoned actresses have also discussed how reality television images of Black women are stereotypical and disheartening. Diahann Carroll, a pioneer in Black women's struggle for media inclusion, said that she refuses to watch reality television. Carroll said, "What I see now on television for the most part is a disgrace, as far as how we're depicted" (Samuels, 2011, para 4).

This discussion among actors mirrors and makes "real" and tangible the findings of researchers who argue that images of Black women in reality television are evidence that the group's struggle with quality media representation has continued (Pozner, 2010). Moreover, depiction of Black women in docusoaps became a hot-button issue and the center of online protests and petitions in 2012. We capture this contention and highlight this pivotal moment in the history of Black women docusoap depictions via a brief analysis of the case of #ENOUGHisENOUGH.

#ENOUGHisENOUGH

Due to popularity and widespread use, the word "hashtag" was added to the *Oxford English Dictionary* in June 2014. The "hashtag" symbol is commonly used on social media sites such as Twitter—a site with more than 271 million monthly active users—as both a form of expression and as a way to categorize users' thoughts. Given the pervasiveness of social media technologies, it should come as no surprise that people turned to the hashtag to share their thoughts and opinions about mediated depictions in reality television. Star Jones—a famous television personality most noted for being one of the original hosts of the ABC weekday morning talk show, *The View*—used the hashtag #ENOUGHisENOUGH after tweeting about her frustrations with the violence exhibited in docusoaps. Her tweet reads, "It may be 'comfortable' to be quiet when women of color slap the crap out of each other & run across tables barefoot, but #ENOUGHisENOUGH" (Scott, 2012, para 3). She then tweets about her decision to take action: "About to put together a group of sisters to finally 'tell the truth' about the image of women of color in the media" (Scott, 2012, para 4). Jones' comments were fueled in part by an episode of *Basketball Wives* (Season 4, Episode 9) where a Latina cast member, Evelyn Lozada, and her Black female assistant, Nia Crooks, attempted to physically attack Black cast member, Jennifer Williams. After Nia slapped Jennifer, both she and Evelyn had to be restrained to prevent more physical contact with Jennifer.

Jones is not the only Black female celebrity to voice her concerns about the portrayals of Black women in *Basketball Wives*. Wendy Williams—a well-known US media personality, actress and author—explained her frustrations with the show: "I don't like to see women fighting, particularly black women fighting…I used to love *Basketball Wives*, I really did." (Popular Critic, 2012, para 5). Viewers were also outraged by the violence shown on *Basketball*

Wives. An online petition, started by Alexis M., called for viewers to boycott *Basketball Wives* because of the violence and bullying among the women. The petition reads, "Evelyn Lozada is a bully. The violence on *Basketball Wives* is horrible and disgraceful. Physical assaults, threats, verbal abuse, and harassment. VH1 is rewarding this behavior by giving Evelyn a spinoff. Don't reward negative behavior" (M., 2012, para 1). The petition garnered over 29,000 signatures. The show, *EV and Ocho*, that Alexis M. proposed boycotting never aired. However, it is interesting to note that at the time *Basketball Wives* continued to air and attract strong viewership.

That episode in Season 4 of *Basketball Wives* was not the only one to be a magnet for criticism. Episode 13 was also heavily discussed in online forums because of the violence and bullying depicted. During a "girls' trip" to Tahiti, a conflict arose between cast members, Tami and Kesha. Tami was called a bully in online discussions and reactions to the show for the way she taunted Kesha, held her pocketbook hostage, and threatened Kesha with physical violence. This was not the first time that Tami engaged in violent behavior on *Basketball Wives*. During her debut season she was involved in conflict with Evelyn Lozada. The ladies had to be separated by cast mates and crewmembers to prevent a physical fight. In Season 3, Tami attacked castmate Meka Claxton in the middle of a nightclub. So, conflict was not new to Tami's character. However, Tami's behavior toward Kesha in Season 4 seemed to be, for many, the proverbial straw that broke the camel's back.

Petitions continued to circulate via the Internet urging viewers to band together and demand that *Basketball Wives* be taken off of the air. Although several of the petitions did not garner as many signatures as Alexis M.'s, each illustrated how viewers were bothered by the images of women (especially Black women) featured in reality television. Moreover, the loss of some advertising support also indicates that certain organizations did not want to be aligned with a show that depicts Black women in this negative way. As a result of some of the public outcry, Tami issued a statement on her Facebook page apologizing for her behavior:

> I don't apologize for it 2b accepted—that is ultimately the other person's right to accept or deny it. My only responsibility is to acknowledge a mistake was made and own up to it. I apologize to my family, my REAL friends, my business colleagues, and my Project Girl ladies 4my recent behavior on BBW. I am NOT a bully as depicted on the show, but I did make poor decisions in handling my differences with my cast mate. I sincerely apologize to all of us, as well as to my castmate who was on the receiving end of my wrath (Black, 2012, para 2).

During the reunion special for Season 4 of *Basketball Wives*, some of the cast members (including Tami Roman) issued apologies for their behavior (Huff Post TV, 2012). Despite the behavior, public response, and loss of advertisers, the show was renewed for a fifth season. After all, despite the petitions, the show still managed to pull in a large number of viewers.

In a summer 2013 issue of *Upscale* magazine, Shaunie (executive producer of *Basketball Wives*) and Tami discussed the upcoming fifth season. The women vowed to provide better representations. In the interview, Shaunie was asked to reflect on viewers' critical responses to the fourth season as well as the loss of some advertising support for the show. Shaunie stated: "[It] was so difficult to deal with when it was airing and when it was all over with. I remember saying, 'what the hell just happened? This isn't us; we're mothers, we're businesswomen. We have to be smarter. We have to represent ourselves a lot better'" (the YBF, 2013, para 5). She also explained how the women agreed it was time for a change: "By the time we did the [Season 4] reunion we all agreed enough is enough. We had a group talk and were all definitely on the same page. We heard the messages loud and clear. We knew we had to do better. It was an eye opener" (the YBF, 2013, para 8). The series continued for a fifth season in 2013. It is presently off the air.

Basketball Wives is only one example of the shows that viewers feel perpetuate negative stereotypes of Black women. As discussed above, several members of the popular press discussed how reality television presented demeaning images—especially the characterization of the "angry Black woman." Petitions have also continued as to other shows that viewers feel will present demeaning images. For example, petitions were circulated to stop production and future airing of *Sorority Sisters* (about Black female sorority members) and *Shawty Lo's All My Babies' Mamas* (about the rapper Shawty Lo, and the 11 children he had with 10 different women). The latter did not make it to the air. *Sorority Sisters*, however, did air on VH1 beginning December 2014. After the premiere episode, many took to social media, saying they were boycotting the show and pressuring advertisers to pull their support.

Images of Black women in reality television (including a spin-off of *Basketball Wives*) were still airing in 2014. Some critics still argued that the images were negative representations of Black women. Moreover, as recently as November 2014 another activist group has emerged challenging Bravo to stop profiting from mediated depictions of Black women fighting (the YBF, 2014). This discussion raises several questions: First, how were Black women depicted in reality television docusoaps (including but not limited to *Basketball Wives*) prior to the public outcry? Did their presentation differ if they were the minority on a predominantly White cast, among the majority on a predominantly Black cast, or cast in the leading role? Second, following the public outcry to *Basketball Wives*, how are Black women depicted in docusoaps—that is, did the outcry have an effect on subsequent images and depictions of Black women? Following the ending of the show, not only have public responses continued about images of Black women in docusoaps, but the apologies and promises issued by the women of *Basketball Wives* introduce a reason to examine Black women's depictions in docusoaps. In this book we seize the opportunity to analyze this phenomenon by analyzing content following #EnoughisEnough.

A Current Gap Being Addressed

The existing literature on women in reality television demonstrates how women are still limited to domestic, subservient, and inferior roles compared to their male counterparts. This genre continues to highlight female participants' physical appearance and reinforce an ideal beauty. Their careers, education, and overall intelligence are either ignored or mocked (e.g., Edwards, 2004; Fairclough, 2004; Graham-Bertolini, 2004; Pozner, 2010; Waggoner, 2004). Pozner (2010) argued that all women experience this hardship; yet, research on Black women in reality television discusses how the images of this group are more troubling than is the case for images of White women.

This book is an extension of and contribution to this ongoing scholarly discussion insomuch as to date no study has focused solely on how Black women are presented in reality television docusoaps despite the fact that researchers have examined race in the docusoaps such as *The Real World* (e.g., Bell-Jordan, 2008; Kraszewski, 2009) and presentations of Black people in docusoaps, among other types of programming (Tyree, 2011). This is a glaring omission because this subgenre has the potential to influence audiences, especially given its hybrid form (whereas documentaries focus on social commentary, docusoaps focus on entertainment) (Bruzzi, 2000; Gillan, 2004). In fact, docusoaps have an especially strong ideological power, one of the most powerful of all reality television subgenres (Biressi & Nunn, 2005) and tend to promote the need for regular exposure to their programs (Holmes, 2004). Such reoccurring exposure can increase their potential power and influence. Hence, docusoaps' popularity and ideological power are reasons why this subgenre and images depicted—especially Black women's roles—warrant further scrutiny.

Tyree's (2011) study in many ways served as an inspiration for this book. Tyree's (2011) analysis illustrated how stereotypical images of Black women still exist in reality television programming, including docusoaps. All but one of the shows Tyree examined featured Black men and women as the minority cast members. In this project, we build upon Tyree's investigation in a few ways. We focus solely on Black women and their presentations in docusoaps and identify shows for analysis where Black women are not in the minority in terms of cast on the show.

We begin this book with an overview of research conducted on Black women's mediated depictions, reality television, and the effects of this source of entertainment. In the next chapter, we discuss the results of our analysis of Black women's depictions in select docusoaps from 2011 in which Black women were members of the majority cast, both as minority members (the Black woman was the numerical minority on the show) and as majority members (the cast was majority Black women). In the next chapter, we discuss the results of our analysis of Black women's depictions in select docusoaps during the 2014 viewing year in which Black women were in the leading role exclusively—for if positive depictions are to occur we should expect them in shows where the Black women are leading characters. We end the book with conclusions, directions for future research, activism, and engagement, and critical reflections on this project.

· 1 ·

BLACK WOMEN'S MEDIATED DEPICTIONS: AN OVERVIEW

In June of 1939, Ethel Waters became one of the first Black people to appear on the then-new medium of television. Her role was that of a warm-hearted maid. This was a significant milestone for Black people; however, more than three decades following Ethel Waters' first appearance on television, Black people's roles on television were still mostly as dedicated domestic workers or unruly savages who were intellectually inferior to White Americans (Gray, 2008; Holtzman & Sharpe, 2004; Smith-Shomade, 2002; Wilson, Gutierrez, & Chao, 2003). These negative, limiting depictions manifested themselves in different forms—especially when depicting Black women. For the purpose of clarity, a brief history of Black women's mediated depictions is provided to ground and situate our current study. After the brief history, we discuss our rationale for discussing Black women's mediated depictions in docusoaps.

Black Women in Media

Black women are considered a "double minority" (Smith-Shomade, 2002, p. 31). More specifically, White (1999) argued that "the uniqueness of the African-American female's situation is that she stands at the crossroads of two of the most well-developed ideologies in America, that regarding women and that regarding the Negro" (p. 27). As a result, Black women have faced and continue to face discrimination and inequality because of their perceived inferiority to both White Americans and men (Byerly, 2007; Collins, 2005; Littlefield, 2008). These ideological implications are only magnified in the realm of entertainment media (Coleman, 2000, 2002, 2003, 2011; Wilson, Gutierrez, & Chao, 2003). For example, Hine (1996) argued that "popular culture is replete with a range of dichotomized images of the good white woman and the evil black woman, the feminine white woman and the masculinized black woman, the chaste, demure, virginal white woman and the sluttish, whorish, depraved black woman, the immoral, unmarried black welfare mother and the dutiful white housewife" (p. 91). Because of such presentations, Douglas (2004) argued that Black women are forced to deal with enlightened sexism in addition to subtle racism.

Prior to the 1960s, Black women were not featured in leading roles. In 1968, however, Diahann Carroll was given the opportunity to play the first Black lead character in a television show. The show, *Julia*, presented a less stereotypical image of a Black woman. The main character, Julia, was cast in a successful job (a nurse) and was depicted as a good mother (Holtzman & Sharpe, 2014; Wilson, Gutierrez, & Chao, 2003). However, even after the success of *Julia*, Black women were more often presented in supporting roles to the White or Black male lead (Smith-Shomade, 2002).

Television representations of Black women increased, most notably beginning in the 1980s (Smith-Shomade, 2002). Both flattering and unflattering images were presented throughout the 1990s, as several sitcoms featuring Black people continued to appear. During this period, Black women appeared in only a few dramas and were mostly limited to television sitcoms and music videos (Douglas, 2004; Holtzman & Sharpe, 2014; Mascaro, 2004; Smith-Shomade, 2002). However, in the 2000s, Black women were given more opportunities to be a part of the main cast of a sitcom (Wilson, Gutierrez, & Chao, 2003). As a result, Black women were beginning to have more freedom in television than ever before (Smith-Shomade, 2002).

Despite these advances in numerical representation, research on televised images of Black women throughout history show that several stereotypes constantly appeared. Smith-Shomade (2002) argued that overall, representations of Black women seemed more one-dimensional than those of White American women. Many of these stereotypes used in television can be traced back to slavery and have been re-presented to adjust to the changing times. Yet, some of the characteristics of the images and the underlying messages about Black people's social value remained the same. The recurring, recycled stereotypical messages continued to objectify Black women (Glascock, 2003; Jewell, 1993; Littlefield, 2008; Mascaro, 2004; Smith-Shomade, 2002; Speight, Thomas, & Witherspoon, 2004). In respect to the instances where Black women were featured in more flattering roles, researchers argued that the empowering messages were still far outnumbered by the demeaning, stereotypical roles (Smith-Shomade, 2002).

In sum, although some images may have empowered Black women, several others were still reinforcing stereotypes and the idea of the group's inferiority (Boylorn, 2008). Hall (2003) argued, "we can grasp [racist images'] recurring resonance better if we identify some of the base-images of the 'grammar of race'" (p. 91). We will assess here whether stereotypical media images are still being recycled in reality television docusoaps. In order to do so, we first discuss these common images and their various forms in order to identify their shared characteristics.

Physical Attractiveness among Black Women

Like all women, Black women are expected to uphold beauty standards. As mentioned earlier, these beauty standards and the need to be physically attractive are communicated through media messages. The definition of beauty varies based on culture (Berry, 2007). Thus, what is considered beautiful among Black people may not be the same for White Americans, Asians, Hispanics, and other ethnicities. Despite the diverse cultural definitions, beauty standards for Black people (as well as other groups) are often based on Eurocentric ideals (Goldman & Waymer, 2014). According to Collins (2009), "African-American women experience the pain of never being able to live up to prevailing standards of beauty—standards used by White men, White women, Black men, and, most painfully, one another" (p. 98). She goes on to argue that these restrictive beauty standards can impact the lives of African American women and have the potential to promote internal and external oppression.

Smith-Shomade (2002) argued, "African-American women are rarely accorded the adjective *beautiful*, either in reference to their physical appearance or their behavior" (p. 117, emphasis in original). She argued that Black women used White standards of beauty as the barometer in evaluating their own attractiveness. In addition, society uses this same system to measure all women's physical appearance. In order to help Black women meet this Eurocentric idea of beauty, as detailed earlier, there are additional ideas communicated about attractive features. For example, traditionally, lighter skin and long, straight (as opposed to a coarser texture) hair are considered the correct or beautiful characteristics. Scholars maintain this is because these two features often closely resemble a White American woman's skin tone and hair (Collins, 2005; Collins, 2009; Smith-Shomade, 2002).

Darker skin is considered less attractive for Black women, as it is the polar opposite of the fair skin of White American women that Eurocentric standards embody as beautiful. This skin tone has also traditionally been attached to other stereotypes and unattractive characteristics (hooks, 2008; Collins, 2009; Smith-Shomade, 2001). For example, Mammy and Sapphire, two historical Black stereotypes considered unattractive or aggressive (respectively), are traditionally dark skinned (Smith-Shomade, 2001). The dark skin tone is often associated with "images of black female bitchiness, evil temper, and treachery"—characteristics also linked to the Sapphire image (hooks, 2008, p. 209).

In addition, being overweight, with short, kinky hair, and strong Afrocentric features are all linked with a dark skin tone and labeled as unattractive by US society and media (Collins, 2009; Smith-Shomade, 2002). Light skin, on the other hand, carries more social value (hooks, 2008). Thus, the ideal for Black women is to have the appropriate distribution of weight (hips, round bottom, breasts) with a lighter skin tone, straight hair, and non-Afrocentric features. If she has a darker skin tone, it is especially important to have more Eurocentric features, such as longer hair, to become more attractive (hooks, 2008; Collins, 2005; Collins, 2009; Smith-Shomade, 2002). Black women who matched these standards were most often featured in television. A question we will return to later is whether these stereotypical depictions continue to exist in reality television docusoaps. Moreover, if these depictions are present how might they be problematized, interrogated, or challenged?

Mammies and Black Ladies

Mammy is a stereotype that dates back to slavery. According to Jewell (1993), "the image of mammy has been the most pervasive of all images constructed by the privileged and perpetuated by the mass media" (p. 37). This character is an example of the contented Black domestic worker. According to European beauty standards, Mammy is unattractive. Historically she was presented as obese and dark skinned, with large buttocks and breasts. Her physical appearance is linked more with masculinity, while her personality and character are linked more to femininity. She is expected to be asexual, faithful, nurturing, and submissive to her White family/employer. The character was also created as a response to more sexualized images of Black women. Harris-Perry (2011) explained, "Black women who labored in white homes had to be reimagined. A seductive, exotic wench would threaten the stability of white families, but an asexual, omnicompetent, devoted servant was ideal" (p. 71). Mammy was able to use aggression, but mostly when it was directed at other Black people or used to protect her White family (Hudson, 1998; Jewell, 1993; McElya, 2007; Pozner, 2010; West, 1995; White, 1999). Her biggest television role came in the 1950s with *The Beulah Show* (Pozner, 2002; Smith-Shomade, 2002).

Collins (2005) argued that the Mammy character "has been resurrected and modernized as a template for middle-class Black womanhood" (p. 140). This modern, revitalized Mammy is often merged with a character that Collins labels the "Black lady" (p. 139). Like the historical Mammy character, this revitalized image still maintains her loyalty to White members of society. She is allowed to use aggression, but only if it is used to gain economic success or for the benefit of others. The Black Lady is also ambitious and professional. Images of the revitalized Mammy and Black Lady began to emerge in television during the 1980s. Collins (2005) argued that the Black Lady was exemplified best by Clair Huxtable of *The Cosby Show*. She is both educated and successful in her career. She is no longer asexual, like the original Mammy, but she still is presented as using her sexuality appropriately. Unlike the historical Mammy, the Black Lady possesses more attractive qualities (Collins, 2005).

Sapphires, Bitches, and Angry Black Women

The Sapphire made her television debut as a character in the 1950s *Amos 'n' Andy* show. This character is nagging, hostile, sassy, and aggressive. Throughout the years, the key physical characteristic of the Sapphire image was a dark skin tone. She mocks Black men for what she considers to be their inadequacies (Collins, 2005; Harris-Perry, 2011; Hudson, 1998; Jewell, 1993; Pozner, 2010; Smith-Shomade, 2002; West, 1995). Jewell (1993) explained, "Because of her intense expressiveness and hands-on-hip, finger-pointing style, Sapphire is viewed as comedic and is never taken seriously" (p. 45). Her sassiness and rudeness contradict with the feminine nature expected of women.

Several characteristics assigned to Sapphire can also be found in a more recent image—the bitch. The bitch "depicts Black women as aggressive, loud, rude, and pushy" (Collins, 2005, p. 123). This character is also criticized for her unjustifiable and constant display of anger (Collins, 2005; Pozner, 2010). The bitch is more confrontational and aggressive than the historical Sapphire. She is also usually portrayed as being a working-class woman. The image has been used in television for several years in order to "defeminize and demonize women while putting them in their place" (Collins, 2005, p. 123). Both Sapphire and the bitch character communicated the idea that Black women were constantly angry, mean, and aggressive.

Collins (2005) discussed how Black women attempted to give the term bitch a more positive spin by relabeling the image as the Black Bitch; both words are intentionally capitalized, unlike "bitch," to help emphasis the more flattering portrayal. The Black Bitch is "super tough and super strong as she uses her looks, sexuality, intellect, and/or aggression in service to African American communities" (p. 124). Unfortunately, this image was not featured continuously by mass media. The few images that did exist were usually found in films of the early 1970s and were not used extensively in television. Instead, television continued to embrace the non-flattering image of the bitch (Collins, 2005).

Promiscuity and Hypersexuality among African American Women

The image of the bitch was extended to another stereotype—the Sexualized Bitch—with close ties to the historical stereotype of Jezebel. The Jezebel character was created out of White men's attempt to justify their practice of sleeping with their Black female slaves. White men painted these women as promiscuous, hypersexual, exotic, and longing for male attention. Jezebel was historically presented as a mulatto woman with European features and therefore considered more attractive than Mammy and Sapphire (Hudson, 1998; Jewell, 1993; Smith-Shomade, 2002; West, 1995; White, 1999). Jezebel contributed greatly to the sexual objectification of Black women (Harris-Perry, 2011; Jewell, 1993; Littlefield, 2008; Smith-Shomade, 2002).

Televised hip-hop videos featuring provocatively dressed Black women especially helped usher in a revitalized Jezebel (Collins, 2005; Littlefield, 2008; Perry, 2003). Collins (2005) termed this new modernized version of the character as the Sexualized Bitch. Like Jezebel, the Sexualized Bitch is among the most popular televised characters of Black women (Collins, 2005). She is most often linked to working class Black women. Several modern images have emerged that continue to present Black women as being hypersexual and promiscuous: They all communicate the underlying theme that Black women are hypersexual and promiscuous. For example, the Freak and the Gold Digger are also linked to promiscuity. The Freak is a Black woman who is sexually "aggressive and wild" (Stephens & Phillips, 2003, p. 21). She often dresses provocatively and enjoys engaging in sexual intercourse with men in order to control them. The Gold Digger also enjoys engaging in promiscuous behavior to obtain financial security and material gain (Stephens & Phillips, 2003). The hypersexuality and promiscuity of different Black female characters transcended into yet another recurring image of Black women—the Bad Black Mother.

Black Motherhood

Because of Black women's perceived hypersexuality and irresponsible sexual behaviors, they were often said to carelessly have a large number of children. Collins (2005) explained, "The thinking behind these images is that unregulated sexuality results in unplanned for, unwanted, and poorly raised children" (p. 130). Kelley (1996) explained how welfare was part of Black single mothers' reality but was far from a luxurious lifestyle. Even with welfare assistance, Black single mothers continued to struggle to feed their families and make a living. Yet, continuous television news coverage of Black women, specifically in the 1980s, discussed these women's heavy dependence on welfare/government assistance in a different light. Focusing on Black mothers who were addicted to crack, rather than on these women's struggles, helped reinforce the idea that most poor and/or working-class women were Bad Black Mothers whose children were destined to fail (Collins, 2005).

Other stereotypical images help communicate the idea that Black women are unfit mothers. The Baby Mama becomes a mother as a result of her hypersexuality. This character is unethical, as she often lies to the father of her children (Stephens & Phillips, 2003). She is usually a "young, single, poor urban [female]" (Tyree, 2009, p. 52). A Black woman can become a Baby Mama intentionally or unintentionally. However, the media normally portray this character as a female who "purposely got pregnant so that she could maintain a relationship, take the man's money, or keep a part of him" (Stephens & Phillips, 2003, p. 34).

Researchers have found that the Matriarch has also been used to present Black women as bad mothers. Although this Black woman is shown working outside of the home to take care of her family, this is sometimes presented in media messages as detrimental to her children. According to White patriarchal values, the Matriarch is defiant as she disobeys traditional gender roles. Instead of tending to her home and children, she spends too much time outside of the home. Therefore, her children's shortcomings and failures are considered to be caused by a lack of proper guidance from their mother (Collins, 1998; Tyree, 2009).

Conversely, other images present Black women as good mothers. As discussed earlier, the Mammy character was presented as a nurturing woman who was often shown caring for and disciplining children. However, she was also presented as being a better and more caring mother figure to the White children of her employer rather than to her own (Collins, 1998; Tyree, 2009). Collins (2005) explained that the revitalized Mammy, the Black Lady, could be credited with being a good mother if she is able to successfully handle her duties inside and outside of the home. Tyree (2009) explained how the Black Lady shares similarities with the Black Queen. This Black Queen is praised for being a good mother who also supports her husband. She is normally a member of the middle class (Reid-Brinkely, 2008; Tyree, 2009). Although all of these images have their own unique features, they also share common characteristics that present Black women as being a good mother or a bad mother.

Dizzy Black Women

Smith-Shomade (2002) identified another recurring image of Black women —the Dizzy Black women. The image draws from past stereotypes of Black women as being idiotic and frantic. Their intellectual inferiority was often threaded within other stereotypical televised images throughout history (Gray, 2008; Holtzman & Sharpe, 2014; Smith-Shomade, 2002; Wilson, Gutierrez, & Chao, 2003). Yet, the actual image of the Dizzy Black woman did not permeate television as much as other images. The character made a few appearances toward the latter part of television history but became more popular starting with sitcoms of the 1990s. This character is a Black version of the dumb blonde image as applied to White American women. Within sitcoms, the Dizzy Black females are featured being taunted by other cast members because of their illogical way of thought processes (Smith-Shomade, 2002).

High Class Divas

Another modern image of Black women is the Diva. Stephens and Phillips (2003) described her as a cocky and high-maintenance Black woman. Her social status labels her as important. She is attractive and seductive but not explicitly sexual. She is not completely dependent on men, as she can earn her own money and material goods. However, the Diva prefers to find a man with high social status and multiple achievements, which add to her own status. Her material belongings and her ability to maintain a luxurious lifestyle mark her status. She needs admiration, and even envy, from those around her.

Stereotypes of Black women have managed to remain present in society through their recycled use in television. The constant portrayal of these shared characteristics communicates certain ideas about Black women. In sum, for years, media representations portrayed Black women as angry Sapphires, promiscuous Jezebels, or nurturing and overweight Mammies (Collins, 2005; Hudson, 1998; Jewell, 1993; West, 1995). Images of Black women showed improvement in quality and quantity following the Civil Rights Movement—when Black people added equal and fair media representation as a goal and fought for justice (Gray, 2008)—but the stereotypes continue to exist in contemporary society—sometimes in a recycled form (Collins, 2005; Entman & Rojecki, 2000). For example, Collins (2005) discussed the sexualized Bitch—a modern version of the historical Jezebel. Although modern versions are not identical to those from the past, the images share certain characteristics and behavior traits. In addition, other stereotypical images of Black women have emerged such as the naïve, illogical Dizzy character (Smith-Shomade, 2002) or the high-maintenance, cocky Diva (Stephens & Phillips, 2003).

One conclusion is clear: Black people in general and Black women specifically have dealt with and continue to deal with limited media inclusion (Byerly, 2007; Collins, 2005; Croteau & Hoynes, 2003; Smith-Shomade, 2002; Wilson, Gutierrez, & Chao, 2003). Compared to media representation of White Americans in general (Glascock, 2003; Wilson, Gutierrez, & Chao,

2003), researchers found that demeaning images of Black people outnumber flattering images (Abraham, 2003; Collins, 2005; Croteau & Hoynes, 2003; Entman & Rojecki, 2000; Hall, 2003; Holtzman & Sharpe, 2014; Wilson, Gutierrez, & Chao, 2003). Most relevant to this study, they found that when Black women are included in television shows, their "double minority" status due to their race and gender (see Smith-Shomade, 2002, p. 31) is most evident in their token status among a mostly all-White cast (Abraham, 2003; Gray, 2004; Haggins, 2001; Wilson, Gutierrez, & Chao, 2003).

With reality television promising a new chance for media inclusion, it is important to see if these shared characteristics still exist in this genre. At the very least, examining images of Black women in reality television adds to the historical overview of their media inclusion. So how are Black women depicted on docusoap shows where they are not the minority versus when they are in the majority? How are they depicted on shows that are supposed to be "representations" of reality?

We can begin to address gaps in the literature by examining images of Black women in docusoaps. First, we need to establish when we define women as "Black" and how we chose to analyze their mediated depictions.

· 2 ·

DOCU-SOAPING BLACK WOMEN

Although there are several genres of reality television—each powerful in its own right—we focus on docusoaps because of their mass appeal. As discussed in the introduction, the docusoap is the most powerful form of reality television (Biressi & Nunn, 2005). Because of its format—similar to a documentary and soap opera and with a recurring cast—audience members are often invested in the docusoap characters' storylines. This format with stories about Black women may have an especially powerful influence on the construction of reality and identity.

Our analysis takes place over two distinct time periods: the 2011 and 2014 viewing seasons. The year 2011–2012 is an important time for analysis because it was directly before the major *Basketball Wives* fallout. To reiterate here, there was an online petition calling for greater accountability of the representations of Black women depicted on the show. During the reunion special for Season 4, some of the cast members issued apologies for their behaviors (Huff Post TV, 2012). Moreover, in a summer 2013 issue of *Upscale* magazine, Shaunie (executive producer of *Basketball Wives*) discussed the upcoming fifth season. The women vowed to provide better representations on the show in what turned out to be the final season. From this incident, we know that negative images of Black women can be found in docusoaps. We hope to dig deeper and add further complexity to this discussion. Thus, one question we seek to establish is whether, prior to the 2012 fallout, differences exist between the mediated representations of Black women in docusoaps with a predominantly Black cast and those that feature Black women as the minority characters?

For the first part of our project (the 2011 viewing year), we analyzed representations of Black women within six popular docusoaps—Bravo's *The Real Housewives of Atlanta*, VH1's *Basketball Wives*, VH1's *Love & Hip Hop*, Oxygen's *Bad Girls Club*, E!'s *Khloe & Lamar*, and MTV's *The Real World*. The first three shows present a cast of mostly Black women, while the latter three feature Black women as the minority cast member. Women were considered Black, if they were labeled as Black, their cast bios classified them as such, or if they were racially ambiguous and could be perceived as Black due to their physical appearance and phenotypical traits. We will discuss the racially ambiguous woman later in this chapter as well as later in the book.

2011 Shows Analyzed

Bravo's *The Real Housewives of Atlanta* is the only show within the *Real Housewives* franchise that features a predominantly African American female cast. It is also the most successful show within the franchise (Nordyke, 2011). In 2011, the show followed the lives of a group of Black women (and one White American woman) who resided in suburban Atlanta, Georgia. In 2011, the show entered its fourth season (BravoTV, 2011), however, the analysis examined the third season, which featured five women (out of a cast of six women) who could be perceived as Black: Nene Leakes, Kandi Burruss, Cynthia Bailey, Phaedra Parks (the newest cast member), and Sheree Whitefield. Following true to docusoaps form, the series followed the women during their everyday lives as they interacted with each other and other members of their social circles. The third season focused on Cynthia's upcoming marriage, Nene's family issues, Sheree's dating life, Kandi's career as a recording artist, and Phaedra's pregnancy. The third season drew in approximately 2.9 million viewers per week.

VH1's *Basketball Wives* followed the lives of a group of predominantly Black women who were the wives, ex-wives, girlfriends, ex-girlfriends, fiancées, or ex-fiancées of current, former, or retired NBA players. Because of its success, VH1 launched a spin-off—*Basketball Wives LA*. The original *Basketball Wives* ended its third season in 2011, and it was announced during the reunion that the show would be renewed for a fourth (and, it turned out, final) season (VH1, 2011a). Season three was used in the analysis. The Black cast members featured during the third season were: Shaunie O'Neal, Royce Reed, Meeka Claxton, Jennifer Williams, and Tami Roman, who made up the majority of the seven-member cast. The season followed the women's everyday lives including an all-women trip to Italy, Jennifer's marital issues, and an introduction to new cast member, Meeka. The premiere of the third season brought in 3.5 million viewers between its original airing and same-day encore episode. The show was so popular VH1 launched a spin-off, *Basketball Wives LA*.

VH1 airs another docusoap that features a cast composed mostly of Black women—*Love & Hip Hop*. The docusoap first aired in 2011 and follows a group of women who have some connection with the hip-hop industry. VH1 announced during the reunion special that the docusoap would be renewed for a second season (VH1, 2011b). The first season of *Love & Hip Hop* was included in our analysis. Out of the five-member cast for the first season, four Black women were presented: Emily Bustamante, Olivia Longott, Chrissy Lampkin, and Mashonda Tifrere. The season introduces the women to the audience and explains their connection to the hip-hop industry. The women are shown interacting with each other and other members of their social circles. The first season averaged more than 1 million viewers, making it quite a success story for VH1 (Williams, 2011). Due to the docusoaps success, VH1 launched spin-off shows *Love & Hip Hop Atlanta* and *Love & Hip Hop Hollywood*.

Oxygen's *Bad Girls Club* is a docusoap that features a group of self-proclaimed bad girls who reside in a house together. Each season, the series follows a different group of women in a different city. The season analyzed—the seventh season—features a group of women in New Orleans (Oxygen, 2011). The docusoap traditionally includes one or two Black females in the predominantly non-Black female cast. In the seventh season, three of the eight cast members could be perceived as Black: Judith "Judi Jai" Jackson, Tiara Hodge, and Nastasia "Stasi" Townsend. The women were followed as they adjusted to one another and their new surroundings. Early on Season 7 was labeled a success for Oxygen, producing "week-over-week ratings growth to season highs." (Seidman, 2011, para 1).

E! aired a docusoap titled *Khloe & Lamar*, which followed reality television star Khloe Kardashian and her NBA player husband Lamar Odom. The show followed the couple in their everyday lives, which included interaction with their family and close friends. The show often featured Khloe's best friend and assistant, Malika Haqq, the only Black female with a recurring role on the show. The docusoap finished its first season successfully in 2011 and began its second season in February 2012 (E! Online, 2011). Malika's presentation in the first season of the docusoap was analyzed. The premiere of Season 1 brought in approximately 1.3 million viewers, ages 18 to 34 (Gorman, 2011).

The last docusoap in the sample was MTV's *The Real World*, which is one of the longest running docusoaps and is often credited for making the genre so popular (Andrejevic, 2004; Moorti & Ross, 2004; Pozner, 2010; Stern, 2005). The show followed seven individuals from different areas as they live and work with each other. Each season features a group of mostly White Americans in a different location. The docusoap began airing its 26th season in September 2011, which followed the group in San Diego, California (MTV, 2011). Since every season does not feature a Black woman, we analyzed season 22—*The Real World–Cancun*—which was, at the time, the last season to feature Black female cast members. The 22nd season featured Jonna Manion and Jasmine Reynaud as they travel to Cancun and move in with their new roommates. The 22nd season of the docusoap was "Wednesday's number one original cable series" (among viewers 12 to 34), sometimes bringing in around 1.8 total viewers (Seidman, 2009, para 1).

We began by compiling a list of all episodes for each of the six docusoaps. Reunion specials were not included as they are not presented in the same narrative structure as the episodes aired during the season. From the compiled lists, three episodes were randomly selected for each docusoap. This resulted in a sample of 18 episodes (See Table 1). Only the recurring Black female characters that were part of the main cast of each series were examined. Thus, the women had to have a biography included on the show's website as part of the main cast biographies. We chose this as a point of emphasis due to the narrative structure of a docusoap, which focuses on the lives of a recurring cast, and focused our analysis on how these recurring cast members are presented to viewers. Within these 18 episodes, 20 Black women were presented in recurring roles. The predominantly Black (PB) female docusoaps featured 14 Black females out of 17 cast members. The predominantly non-Black (PNB) female docusoaps featured 6 Black females out of 19 cast members.

Table 1. 2011 Docusoaps Episodes Analyzed: Predominantly Black Women Casts and Predominantly Non-Black Women Casts.

DOCUSOAP	EPISODES	LIST OF CHARACTERS
The Real Housewives of Atlanta (PB)	#2 – Model Behavior #4 – Petty Boughetto #14 – Flamingo Roadblock	Nene, Cynthia, Phaedra, Kandi, Sheree
Basketball Wives (PB)	#2 #7 #8 Note: Episodes for this docusoap did not have titles—only episode numbers.	Jennifer, Shaunie, Tami, Royce, Meeka
Love & Hip Hop (PB)	#2 – The Birthday #3 – The Yacht #8 – Me Against the Joneses	Mashonda, Olivia, Chrissy, Emily
The Real World–Cancun (PNB)	#3 #8 #11	Jonna, Jasmine
Bad Girls Club–New Orleans (PNB)	#5 – Playing for the Other Team #6 – Better off Dread #10 – Truces, Tirades and Tiaras	Nastasia, Judi, Tiara
Khloe & Lamar (PNB)	#1 – The Father-in-Law #4 – The Break-Up #8 – Baby Blues	Malika

All cast biographies were accessed from the docusoaps' websites. Notes were taken on how the women were described in their cast biographies. We also viewed each of the 18 episodes and took detailed notes about the depicted images of the 20 Black women featured in the docusoaps. This method helped us in addressing the question mentioned earlier: Prior to the 2012 fallout, did differences exist between the mediated representations of Black women in docusoaps with a predominately Black cast and those that feature Black women as the minority characters? Additionally, we took notes on elements of analysis discussed in Tyree's (2011) study on Black people in reality television. In explaining the procedure, Tyree wrote:

Each participant was analyzed to identify any "physical confirmations" of stereotypical behavior, which included a participant's appearance, gestures, movements, and actions. Verbal confirmations of stereotypical dialogue [were] also analyzed, including whether participants spoke slang, phrases, or words that could solidify their categorization within specific stereotypes. Another key component of the analysis was the identification of behaviors or dialogue by other cast members that framed the participant as a specific stereotype (p. 402).

Tyree's procedure revealed the importance of examining the character's behaviors and dialogue in order to see if they aligned with behaviors associated with different stereotypes. In addition, the procedure illustrates the importance of looking for explicit labeling of Black women as specific stereotypes. Inspired by Tyree's research, we listed seven elements on a data collection form:

1. Storylines that the Black female cast members were involved in
2. Interactions between a Black female cast member and other cast members
3. Dialogue about a Black female cast member and her behaviors
4. Actions and behaviors exhibited by a Black female cast member
5. Characteristics and personality traits of the Black female cast members
6. Physical appearance of the Black female cast members
7. Black female identified as stereotype (by herself or other cast member)

After this initial viewing and note-taking, we first viewed the episodes again while revisiting the notes, and we added any information that was not noted in the first round of viewing. During a third round of viewing, we transcribed direct quotes from the Black cast members and their cast mates. Quotes were selected that aligned with the notes made on each of the elements discussed earlier.

2014 Episodes Analyzed

In the second part of our project (2014 viewing season), we analyzed docusoaps with Black women as leading cast members. It is key that we note that many networks have included reality television in their line-up—some more than others. After a systematic review of major cable networks' websites and their program listings, we found five networks at which at least 50% of their original reality television programming was made up of docusoaps—TLC,

Bravo, Oxygen, WE tv, and VH1. TLC was subsequently eliminated from analysis of the second portion of our analysis because the current docusoaps listed did not include Black women as the leading characters. Across the remaining four networks as of June 2014, there were 41 docusoaps listed. Our goal was to look at the most recent representations of Black women, so we narrowed the list to only include 2014 seasons that had finished airing all episodes (excluding reunion specials) by August 2014. In the event that the docusoap had one season airing in both 2013 and 2014, the docusoap was included if the majority (51%) of the episodes aired in 2014. We also focused on docusoaps that featured at least two Black women in the main cast and/or recurring role. This resulted in 15 docusoaps. See Table 2 for a complete list of the shows for each network.

Table 2. List of 2014 Docusoaps Analyzed.

WE tv	BRAVO	OXYGEN	VH1
Mary Mary (Season 3)	The Real Housewives of Atlanta (Season 6)**	Bad Girls Club, Chicago (Season 12)	Basketball Wives LA (Season 3)
SWV Reunited (Season 1)	Kandi's Wedding (Season 4)		Love & Hip Hop Atlanta (Season 3)
Marriage Boot Camp (Season 2)	Married to Medicine (Season 2)		Marrying the Game (Season 3)
Marriage Boot Camp: Reality Stars (Season 1/Season 3*)	Blood, Sweat, and Heels (Season 1)		Hollywood Exes (Season 3)
L.A. Hair (Season 3)			La La's Full Court Life (Season 5)***

*Marriage Boot Camp: Reality Stars is sometime referred to as the third season of Marriage Boot Camp. However, both shows were included in the analysis because each is listed on WE tv's list of current shows.
**Season 6 of The Real Housewives of Atlanta began airing in 2013 and continued through 2014. It was included in the analysis since the majority of the episodes (more than 70%) aired in 2014.
***Although La La does not see herself as exclusively a Black woman, she was included in the analysis for our discussion on racial ambiguity and the social construction of race because of viewers' perceptions of her race.

Four hours of airtime were randomly selected from each docusoap. In other words, four shows were selected if the docusoaps ran for 60 minutes;

8 episodes were selected for docusoaps that ran for 30 minutes. Only regular episodes were considered; reunions and other specials were not used since they do not follow the same narrative structure as the regular episodes. In total, we examined 68 episodes, or approximately 60 hours of footage. Each Black female cast member featured in the episodes as part of the storyline was examined. A female was determined to be "Black" if she appeared to be Black phenotypically and was not identified as otherwise. This is consistent with Dubrofsky's (2011) argument of racial ambiguity, which she used in her analysis of *The Bachelor*. She argued that reality television shows may feature a woman of color whose appearance is ambiguous enough so that she *appears* to be a specific race even if she is not explicitly labeled as such. Thus, that character can serve as a representative of any racial group to which the audience believes she belongs.

Two of the defining characteristics of docusoaps are a continuing storyline and recurring characters. In order to fully understand the representations of Black women within these shows, it is important to consider the context of each docusoap. To help with this, we preface our analysis with a brief description of each show, which includes the history of the shows, their viewership, and their characters.

Descriptions of the Docusoaps Analyzed

WE tv

WE tv's *Mary Mary* follows the lives of the gospel-singing duo of the same name, which consists of sisters Erica Campbell and Tina Campbell. The 2014 season marked the third year for the docusoap. Throughout the series, viewers learn more about the women's personal and professional lives. Key storylines in the season include Tina's husband's infidelity and Erica's desires to pursue a solo career. Although the show centers on the lives of Erica and Tina, there are also frequent appearances by other Black women, especially their sister and stylist, who is affectionately known as Goo Goo. According to EURWEB (2014), parent company to WE tv, "The show delivered more than 1.1 million total viewers, up +46% over the previous season, with strong growth in the key adult and women demos…*Mary Mary* helped make WE tv a top five cable network on Thursday nights among women 18–49 and 25–54, and was the #1 show among African American adults and women 18–49 and 25–54, excluding sports" (para 2–3).

SWV Reunited chronicles the reunion and touring of the popular 90s singing group SWV, composed of members Cheryl "Coko" Clemons, Tamara "Taj" Johnson-George, and Leanne "Lelee" Lyons. The show began in 2014 and featured two seasons within that year. The first season was used for the analysis because it was completed, but the second season had not finished airing at the time of our research. The show follows the women as they work together to rebuild their friendship and career. The women are also shown interacting with own children and other family members. The show "averaged 1.2 million viewers over its initial six-episode run" (Friedlander, 2014, para 3).

Marriage Boot Camp is a follow-up of sorts to a different popular reality television show aired on WE tv—*Bridezillas*. Some of the bridezillas and their husbands are invited to the *Marriage Boot Camp* series in order to work on their relationships. Their troubled marriages may not be too shocking to viewers since the women's stint on *Bridezillas* featured the brides-to-be exhibiting unruly and aggressive behaviors—often toward their husbands, family, and bridal party. The show first aired in 2013 with record-breaking ratings for WE tv. According to their website, the show was "renewed for a second season after helping to make WE tv the #1 women's network for young women on Friday nights" (We Tell All, 2013). Two Black women were featured—Gloria Darrington and LaTashijuna "Tasha" Daniel—as they worked on their relationships with their husbands.

As a follow-up to the series, WE tv also launched *Marriage Boot Camp: Reality Stars* in 2014. Instead of former bridezillas, the show features reality television stars whose relationship problems had been previously highlighted in a different reality show. The series featured two Black female reality stars—Traci Braxton of *Braxton Family Values* and Tanisha Thomas who was first introduced in the second season of *Bad Girls Club*. The show proved successful for the network: "The premiere of WE tv's *Marriage Boot Camp: Reality Stars* enjoyed its highest ever franchise debut, delivering more than 1.3 million total viewers to the network during its premiere on Friday night, plus three days of DVR playback" (AMC Networks, 2014, para 1). The docusoap is sometimes referred to as Season 3 of *Marriage Boot Camp*. However the reality stars version was included as well as the original version of the show since both "series" are separate shows on the WE tv website.

Celebrity hair stylist Kim Kimble is the subject of the series, *L.A. Hair*. Viewers tune in and learn about Kim's work with her different clients and her interactions with her team, which includes her mother, Jasmine "Jas" Kimble, and her sister (and salon manager) Leah Aldridge. The show also features other Black women on a consistent basis including hair stylists China Upshaw and Angela Christine Stevens (the latter no longer works in the Kimble salon). During the season, viewers watch as Kim attempts to expand her business in the midst of personal conflicts in her salon. The show has been a rising star for WE tv. According to a WE tv press release, "Over its debut season, the show's sophomore average grew an impressive +66% among W25–54, +40% among W18–49 and +57% among both total viewers and total women" (WE tv, 2013, para 2). This success led WE tv to renew the show for a third season, which aired in 2014.

Bravo

Bravo's *The Real Housewives of Atlanta*—discussed earlier—was analyzed again in the 2014 study. The show aired its sixth and seventh season in 2014. The sixth season was used in our analysis as the seventh season had not yet begun at the start of our research. This particular season began in 2013 and ended in 2014. However, the majority of the episodes (17/22, excluding reunions and specials) were aired in 2014. The sixth season focused on the lives of six Black women: Nene Leakes, Kandi Burruss, Cynthia Bailey, Phaedra Parks, Kenya Moore, and Porsha Stewart (who re-adopts her maiden name, Williams, following her divorce). Other Black women were also featured occasionally, such as Kandi's mother Joyce "Momma Joyce" Jones. The season focuses on topics such as Porsha's divorce from former football player Kordell Stewart; Phaedra's marital issues with her husband, Apollo, who is rumored to have an inappropriate relationship with cast member Kenya; and Kandi's attempt to mediate the hostile relationship between her mother and fiancé. According to Access Atlanta, a segment of *The Atlanta Journal-Constitution*, during the 2014 season "the Bravo reality show that won't stop hit a new milestone: 4.52 million viewers in first viewing. That's the highest number of overnight viewers since the show debuted, beating a season 3 reunion show which drew nearly 4.4 million viewers" (Ho, 2014, para 2).

Kandi was given a spin-off to *The Real Housewives of Atlanta* with the first season airing in 2014. The show, *Kandi's Wedding*, followed Kandi and her staff, family, and friends, as they prepared for her upcoming nuptials. The tension between Kandi's mother and fiancé continued to be a big storyline. Other Black women were also featured in the show including Kandi's mom, assistant, aunts, and bridal party. *Kandi's Wedding* had the most successful premiere night of all *The Real Housewives of Atlanta* spin-offs. According to a July 2014 press release from Bravo Media on parent company NBC Universal's website, "New series *The Real Housewives of Atlanta: Kandi's Wedding*…[was] averaging 1.6 million P18–49 and over 2.8 million total viewers. The series premiere on June 1 earned 1.7 million P18–49 and 3.1 million total viewers making it the network's highest-rated series premiere among all key demos…" (BravoMedia, 2014, para 3).

Married to Medicine first began in 2013, with its second season airing in 2014. The series focuses on women in or related to the medical industry. Black female stars of the show include Drs. Heavenly Kimes, Jackie Walters, and Simone Whitmore and physicians' wives Toya Bush-Harris, Mariah Huqq, and Quad Webb-Lunceford. Mariah's mother and sister also frequently appear on the show. It is important to note that Lisa Nicole Cloud was also featured on the show in the main cast. She is a racially ambiguous character but was not identified as a Black woman. She is discussed later in our chapter on racial ambiguity. The second season focused heavily on the women's business ventures—Jackie's desire for children, Simone's financial troubles, and the failed friendship between Mariah and Quad. According to a July 2014 BravoMedia press release, "season 2 of *Married to Medicine* [was] averaging 1.1 million P18–49 and 2 million total viewers" (BravoMedia, 2014, para 3).

Blood, Sweat, and Heels follows the lives of acquaintances Melyssa Ford, Brie Blythewood, Daisy Lewellyn, Mica Hughes, Demetria Lucas, and Geneva Thomas. The first season aired in 2014; "Bravo's highest rated series premiered on 1/05/14 and [averaged] 2 million total viewers for its first season" (NBC Universal, 2014, para 4). The show featured the women's friendships and conflicts. The show also follows each woman on her career path, including Demetria's successful blog and upcoming book and Melyssa's transition from video vixen to real estate agent.

Oxygen

Oxygen's *Bad Girls Club* is another popular docusoap used for the 2014 analysis. The twelfth season of the series aired in 2014 and followed a group of women living in Chicago. A thirteenth season aired in 2014, inviting past "bad girls" back and giving them a chance to redeem themselves. However, that season was not used in the analysis, as it was not completed at the time of our research. The fact that it is in its thirteenth season speaks to the success of the show. Between original cast members and cast replacements, the twelfth season featured five Black women—Alexandria "Alex/Slim" Rice, Alyssa "Redd" Carswell, Jonica "Blu" Booth, Loren "Lo" Jordan, and Raesha Clanton. The women were followed as they adjusted to one another and their new surroundings.

VH1

VH1's *Basketball Wives LA* began in 2011 and follows the lives of a group of women who are the wives, ex-wives, girlfriends, ex-girlfriends, fiancées, or ex-fiancées of a current, former, or retired NBA basketball player. As discussed earlier, the show was created as a spin-off to *Basketball Wives*. Like the original, the spin-off also experienced some success. So much so that the third season aired in 2014 and featured five main cast members, all of whom are Black—Jackie Christie, Draya Michele, Malaysia Pargo, Brittish Williams, Brandi Maxwell, and Sundy Carter. Major story themes include Draya's new relationship, Brandi's infertility issues due to her battle with cancer, and ongoing feuds between different Black female cast members such as Sundy and Brandi.

VH1 airs another docusoap that features a cast made up mostly of Black women—*Love & Hip Hop Atlanta*. The docusoap first aired in 2012 as a spin-off to the original show, *Love & Hip Hop*, which was used in the 2011 study. During 2014, the third season aired, featuring Black cast members Mimi Faust, Rasheedah Bruckner-Frost, Erica Dixon, Karlie Redd, Tammy Rivera, Ariane Davis, and Kalenna Harper. Although not included on VH1's cast page for the show, there are also frequent appearances from other Black women including Deborah "Momma Dee" Bryant, Althea Heart, Erica Pinkett, Adiz "Bambi" Benson, and Debra "Deb" Antney. The series focuses heavily on the women's friendships and romantic relationships. A major topic of discussion in the current season is Mimi's recently released sex tape. The premiere of the third season brought in 5.6 million viewers (between the original air and rerun) and "also yielded a total of 33 trends on Twitter, with 257,540 unique tweeters producing a total of 1.66 million tweets" (Black, 2014, para 5).

Marrying the Game first aired in 2012. The show was originally created to follow Tiffney Cambridge and her fiancé, famed rapper Jayceon "The Game" Taylor, prepare for their wedding. Because of the success of the show, VH1 continued with the series even though the wedding was called off. In 2014, the third season focused on the official break-up of the couple and the aftermath. The analyzed season featured Tiffney gaining her independence. Viewers watched her adjust to her new relationship status and co-parenting in different homes apart from her ex-fiancé. Although not included on the show's main page, other Black women are occasionally featured on the show including Tiffney's friends, her sister, and The Game's personal assistant.

Hollywood Exes began in 2012 documenting the lives of a group of women who were once married to celebrities. In 2014, the show aired its third season. Four of the cast members were Black women—Nicole Murphy, Sheree Fletcher, Andrea "Drea" Kelly, and Shamicka Lawrence. The women's friendship was highlighted through the series, in addition to discussions of the women's identities outside of their celebrity exes. The show also focused heavily on Andrea's upcoming wedding. The third season contributed to VH1's success: "VH1 notched a strong and significant performance on Wednesday nights for the quarter—increasing primetime impressions by 104% compared to the same quarter in 2013. Growth was fueled by such series as season 3 of 'Hollywood Exes' which is pacing up +28% versus the same number of episodes in season 2" (TV by the Numbers, 2014, para 7).

But She Isn't Black? Or Is She?

Two of the women viewed were also analyzed in relationship to each other and separately from the other Black women—La La and Mica. However, each still plays a role in the narrative of Black women in docusoaps. La La is the leading lady of the VH1 docusoap, *La La's Full Court Life*. The show follows La La in her personal and business life. She is often shown interacting with other female associates, especially her friend Po Johnson and cousin Candice "Dice" Dixon. In the fifth season La La is in the process of launching a new clothing line while still maintaining her other business and personal obligations. In her personal essay titled, "Yo Soy Boricua," La La explains her racial background and identifies herself as Latina. She also addresses people's comments about her race, including some people's original assumption that she was Black. She writes,

> A lot of people don't realize that I'm Latina, which is fine. One thing about being Latina is that there isn't one look that comes with the territory. I don't expect people to know my cultural background just by glancing at me. I do, however, expect that when I tell people my family is from Puerto Rico, that I will be believed and not accused of trying to be something that I'm not. It usually goes something like this: a person having a conversation with me discovers one way or another that I'm Puerto Rican and fluent in Spanish. That person then expresses their shock over these realizations for any number of reasons—common responses are, "You don't look Latina" and "I thought you were black!" I never said I wasn't black. And since when does being black and being Latina have to be mutually exclusive? (Vazquez, 2010, para 1).

La La's essay brings up a couple of interesting points relevant to our discussion of Black women in docusoaps. First, she touches on how some of her fans view her as a representation of Black women. This could be due to her appearance but it also may also be impacted by her career and other acquaintances. For example, La La is married to popular Black NBA player Carmello Anthony and was featured in two popular films with a predominantly Black cast, *Think Like a Man* and *Think Like a Man Too*. Numerous scholars have documented the blurring boundaries of racial/ethnic categorizations where Latino or Hispanic might be deemed as unifying ethnic categories for persons of Spanish descent, yet the social construction of race (as perceived biological differences based on phenotypical traits) serves to privilege some, disadvantage others, and essentially distinguish White Latinos from non-White Latinos (Vargas, 2008).

> Puerto Rico's approach to racial issues can be described as a "conspiracy of silence." It is the issue no one dares to talk about…Puerto Ricans talking about race is a cause for embarrassment, amazement, ambivalence, and silence. For Puerto Ricans race is a matter of "skin pigmentation, facial features, and hair texture, regardless of their ancestry.… there are at least nineteen different racial categories: blanco, blanquito, colorao, rubio, cano, jincho, blanco con raja, jabao, trigueño moreno, mulatto, indio, café conleche, piel canela, prieto, grifo, de color, negro, negrito… Puerto Ricans have developed an elaborate racist vocabulary to refer to racially stereotyped characteristics—especially the idea that kinky hair is 'bad' (pelo malo)" (p. 245). All of these categories reinforce race as a signifier that is determined primarily by the eye. (Vargas, 2008, p. 942)

Given the complexities of race as indicated above, the notion of race as a social construction is discussed in more detail later in the book. Thus, due to her statements about her own racial/ethnic characterizations, La La could also be viewed as an example of the racially ambiguous woman of color featured in media because she was often accused of not *looking* Puerto Rican. Thirdly, La La does not fully separate herself from being Black.

For those reasons, La La's presentations in reality television were also considered in our examination. Because she does identify herself as Puerto Rican, she is not included in the general discussion of Black women in docusoaps. However, her representations are examined and reported in another chapter that specifically considers her role as a racially ambiguous character and how she fits into the equation of portrayals of Black women in docusoaps.

Mica Hughes, one of the cast members from Bravo's *Blood, Sweat, and Heels*, is a model and esthetician (a person licensed to deliver beauty and health care services such as facials and make-up application). Throughout the season viewers learn more about her relationship with her boyfriend, the loss of her father, and conflicts with other cast members over what some of the ladies consider to be her drinking problem and erratic behavior. In addition, Mica is a racially ambiguous character. In fact, Mica was not initially included on the list of Black women to analyze because of her appearance. We did not originally perceive her as a Black woman. Although she did not write an essay about her ethnicity and does not have the same celebrity status as La La, she still has a unique appearance that must be considered in our discussion. In one episode of the docusoap, Mica's mother visits—she appears to be Black.

In an interview with Chris Witherspoon (2014) of theGrio, Mica identifies herself as Black. Witherspoon writes, "Mica later set the record straight on her ethnicity, which has been debated amongst several media outlets. 'Both of my parents are black,' she said. 'I am an African-American woman.' She also recalled a story where a white woman told her she was 'much too beautiful to be black'" (para 8–9). The episodes were revisited and Mica was included in the analysis. Mica's statements illustrate how her racial ambiguity led people to label her as a different race. Since Mica is self-identified as a Black woman, she was included in the analysis of other Black female cast members. However, she is also included in our discussion about the role of racially ambiguous characters in Black women media depictions in docusoaps. Other women of color who could also be viewed as racially ambiguous are also discussed later. Although these women did not make social public statements about their race like La La and Mica, their appearance and presence in the docusoaps could possibly add to the conversation on Black women in reality television.

Deconstructing the Women's *Reality*

Notes were taken on the behaviors, interactions, and appearances of each Black female cast member included in an episode. Each episode was viewed twice in order to ensure thorough, accurate notes were taken. In our note-taking process, we analyzed the communication and interactions among Black female cast members and others. After all of the shows were viewed, we categorized the notes based on common themes. Consistent with Tyree's (2011) analysis of reality television docusoaps, traditional stereotypical images of

Black women were considered when reviewing the notes collected. This helped to show if the women's behaviors mimicked any historical or more recent stereotypical depictions. Lastly, we looked for relationships among the themes to help draw larger conclusions about the representations of Black women in docusoaps. In doing so, we also discussed the potential implications of such representations for individual viewers and society, as a whole.

In sum, we argue that reality television makes a false promise to present reality to its audiences and, like all media messages, has the power to educate its audiences on how to think and behave. Considering this potential, we use Berger and Luckmann's (1967) Social Construction of Reality framework to help assess the potential meaning and power of the current images of Black women in docusoaps. According to social constructionists, individuals use information from social institutions to help construct their ideas about the real world. Mass media serve as an example of such social institutions that individuals use in connection with other sources (Baran & Davis, 2009).

Researchers have also used the Social Construction of Reality framework to help illustrate how reality television constructs ideas about different topics, such as fatherhood (Smith, 2008) and female relationships (Chittenden, 2011). We use the theoretical framework in this book to determine how reality television docusoaps present images of Black women as well as to determine what images were constructed via docusoaps. We also consider and discuss the ways in which this constructed reality could impact audience members' construction of reality. While analyzing these images, we drew upon research on images of Black women (as highlighted above) to determine if and how these stereotypical images persist in docusoaps.

· 3 ·

DOES MAJORITY OR MINORITY CAST STATUS MATTER?

The question in this chapter is: "How do the mediated representations of Black women in docusoaps in which they are featured in a predominantly Black (PB) female cast differ from those that feature Black women as the minority (PNB) characters"? In our analysis of the 2011 season of the shows mentioned in Chapter 2, we found that differences do exist, as some dominant categories for Black women in the PB shows did not emerge as dominant categories for the Black women in the PNB shows. These dominant categories, which emerged from the narrated lived experiences of 14 Black women in the PB shows were: the Professional Black Woman (n=13), the Good Black Mother (n = 10), and the High Class Black Woman (n = 14). Each of these images was presented overall in a flattering light.

There there was one category that emerged as a dominant character for the Black women in the PNB shows only. Five of the six Black women in the PNB shows were presented as the Sexualized Black Woman. The character was presented in an unflattering light. Table 3 illustrates how these images appeared in PB shows compared to the PNB shows.

Table 3. Differences Between 2011 PB Docusoaps and PNB Docusoaps.

	PB Shows (Out of 14)	PNB (Out of 6)
The Professional Black Woman	13	1
The Good Black Mother	10	0
The High Class Black Woman	14	0
The Sexualized Black Woman	0	5

Of note is the way in which physical attractiveness was communicated. The presentation of this constructed image differed in the PB shows and the PNB shows. Moreover, the women's use of the label Bitch also differed based on the cast composition. For example, while the PB shows used the term more often as a derogatory label (seven out of nine instances), the PNB shows used the term more as a positive label (nine out of twelve instances). Thus, indeed there were differences in the way Black women from the PB docusoaps were presented compared to way Black women were depicted in the PNB docusoaps. Below we detail these differences.

The Professional Black Woman

The majority (92%) of the Black women in the PB shows were presented as being professional, ambitious women with successful careers. Each of these qualities fit into the Professional Black Woman category. However, cast biographies were more likely to present this character (the Professional Black Woman) than what was actually depicted in the episodes. More specifically, this image was communicated in thirteen of the fourteen women's cast biographies; however, it was only exhibited in an actual episode by seven of the 14 women. In these seven instances, the women were shown speaking about their success or working in their profession. When the Professional Black Woman was featured, she was presented in a flattering light. The Professional Black Woman was only exhibited by one of the six PNB participants; it was not a dominant category.

Cast biographies presented the Professional Black Woman in the PB shows by describing the women's successful careers. For example, *Love & Hip Hop* cast member Olivia's biography mentioned her success as a music artist. The biography also touched on her ambition: "Her pursuit and love of music will cement her within the industry for years to come. She will continue to prove that she has numerous talents to show the world." Olivia was also shown pursuing her musical career in the show.

Love & Hip Hop cast member Emily's biography also discussed her successful career. The biography noted: "…Emily quickly developed a reputation as one of the most respected and sought after fashion stylists in the entertainment business." Emily was also featured in one of the episodes discussing her job as a stylist. As another example of this category, Jennifer from *Basketball Wives* was described as "a high-end real estate agent and wildly successful business owner of the upscale women's work out company Flirty Girl Fitness." Fellow cast member Tami was described in her cast biography as a woman who "has a string of acting credits under her belt and currently pays the bills with her day job as a financial executive."

An example of the Professional Black Woman in action was found in an episode of *The Real Housewives of Atlanta*. Cast member Kandi was commended for being a successful music artist. While working in the music studio with Kandi, writer and musical artist Neyo commented, "Kandi's a very prolific songwriter. She's written a bunch of hits for a bunch of different people…I'm honored to be working with her." Kandi is shown actively working and is complimented by a fellow professional in the field. Kandi also referenced her own success in the introductory scene of the show when she stated, "I have fame and fortune, and I've earned it." Phadera, another cast member from *The Real Housewives of Atlanta*, is also depicted as a Professional Black Woman. In the show she referred to herself as "an attorney to the stars"; she was also featured in an episode working in her law office with a client.

The Good Black Mother

Ninety-two percent of the Black women in the PB shows were mothers. None of these women was presented as a bad or unfit mother. Instead, the women's children were mentioned; they were shown interacting with their children; or they were described as selfless and nurturing caregivers. These qualities align with the Good Black Mother category. The image was communicated more often within cast biographies than throughout the actual episodes. Ten of the 14 women were presented as mothers within their biographies. Yet, only four of the 14 women were shown fulfilling their duties as a good mother. None of the six women from the PNB shows was presented as a mother.

The Good Black Mother was presented in *The Real Housewives of Atlanta* by Cynthia, Nene, Sheree, and Kandi. For example, Cynthia was shown interacting with her daughter. It appears as if they were having quality time together. Nene is shown disciplining her son, Bryson, while explaining that her reason for being so stern was because of how much she cared for him. Sheree was shown helping her children pack as they prepared to go visit their father. Each of these examples presented the Black women in their role as mothers, helping and interacting with their children. Kandi was also featured interacting with her daughter. While singing in the recording studio, Kandi asked her producer to stop the music temporarily so she could answer an incoming phone call from her daughter. During the phone conversation she was shown assisting her daughter (by telling her where to find her stuffed animal) while also disciplining her (by telling her she needed to be in the bed at that late hour). Kandi's attention to her daughter, despite her work schedule, communicated how she was able to serve as a mother and professional. This ability to multitask without it interfering with her job as a mother is a characteristic of the Good Black Mother. Expectant mother Phaedra from *The Real Housewives of Atlanta* also exhibited the ability and willingness to both work and be a mother. She is filmed saying, "I love what I do. And even though I'm about to have this baby, I don't plan on slowing down in my career one bit."

The cast biographies portrayed the women as good mothers. For example, Shaunie from *Basketball Wives* was described as a "devoted mother." Tami, also from *Basketball Wives*, was described as a woman who "did what she thought was best for herself and for her girls." *Love & Hip Hop* cast member, Mashonda, was discussed as a mother in her cast biography: "Mashonda admits that her number one priority is her [three]-year-old son Kasseem Jr." In each of these examples, the women are described as being devoted to their top priority, i.e., their children. According to Emily's (*Love & Hip Hop*) biography, she became a mother at a young age. However, she was not presented as an irresponsible teen mother. Her biography stated: "…unlike many teen mothers, instead of derailing her plans for success, she became even more determined to find her own identity and make her dreams come true." She was described as a young mother who still pursued her career goals. Her ability to focus on her dreams and her child is characteristic of the Good Black Mother.

The High Class Black Woman

All 14 of the Black women in the PB shows were presented as members of the upper class. The women were shown to be maintaining a very expensive life style. This was exhibited through their social status, material possessions, and social activities. In all three of the PB docusoaps, the women were shown engaging in several activities that could be considered luxurious and expensive. For example, all five of the women in *The Real Housewives of Atlanta* took a trip to Miami, Florida, for a bachelorette party and getaway. In *Basketball Wives*, four of the five women took a week-long trip to Italy. Three of the four women from *Love & Hip Hop* enjoyed a day at the spa. These are all activities that lower-income individuals would not be able to afford.

The PB cast members were also presented as having a higher social status because of their relationships (past or present) and professions. For example, all five women in *Basketball Wives* and all four women in *Love & Hip Hop* were featured as having ties in two popular and lucrative industries—basketball and hip hop, respectively. Connection with these high-powered lifestyles displayed the women as being upper class and having correspondingly expensive lifestyles. In addition, the women's professions implied that they were well off. For example, Cynthia from *The Real Housewives of Atlanta* was a successful supermodel—a career that showered her with money, popularity, and social status. Phaedra's (*The Real Housewives of Atlanta*) career as an entertainment attorney indicated her financial independence and high social status.

This image of the High Class Black Woman was not presented in the PNB shows. When the women were presented taking part in luxurious and expensive activities, it was presented as being a part of the show's storyline, not the women's lifestyles. For example, all three of the Black women in *Bad Girls Club New Orleans* were living in a mansion (with their other roommates) and often using a limousine to visit the local nightclubs. However, audience members were aware that these items were only awarded to the women as long as they were participating on the show. For example, the show's logo was featured prominently on the door of the limousine and in several parts of the house. Thus, although the women were shown enjoying luxury items, it is clear that those items and that lifestyle are not a result of their permanent status or economic standing.

The Sexualized Black Woman

The majority (83%) of the women in the PNB shows were presented as hypersexual. The women's actions and dialogue communicated their promiscuity and their casual attitudes toward sex. Their promiscuity was also discussed by other cast members or obvious in their cast biographies. They all fit into the Sexualized Black Woman category—an unflattering presentation as their sexuality was expressed casually and irresponsibly. None of the women from the PB shows was presented in this manner.

Judi, from *Bad Girls Club: New Orleans*, was presented as the Sexualized Black Woman. In one episode, she had been having a conversation with a man at a nightclub and as she was shown walking out of the club with him, the audience hears Judi saying, "I do like this guy. And by the way, we all are not exactly sure what his name is, but I already know I'm going to have sex with this boy. Don't judge me." The fact that she is unaware of the man's name indicates her lack of any need for a relationship. Her willingness to have sex with him at this point illustrated the irresponsible sexual behavior of the Sexualized Black Woman.

Judi's promiscuous behavior was celebrated and criticized by cast members. For example, Shelley—who was often shown feuding with Judi—commented: "Seriously, Judy. Bringing dudes home and even hooking up on the first night that you met them. That's just tacky and goes to show how you feel about yourself. And obviously, you don't have high standards for yourself." Yet in a different scene, Judi's friends jokingly tease her about having sexual intercourse with more than one guy during their time in New Orleans:

> Angelique: Judy, you've had [sex with] two [guys] already!
> Nastasia: I'm trying to catch up with Judy, ok?

Here, the ladies do not frame Judi's actions negatively. Instead, Nastasia is envious. Nastasia's comment also communicates hypersexuality. As a Black woman, she is expressing her desire to have sex with multiple men like Judi.

Tiara from *Bad Girls Club: New Orleans* was another example of the Sexualized Black Woman. Her cast biography explained that Tiara is a self-proclaimed Gold Digger who is "on the prowl for her next sugar daddy." As discussed earlier, the Gold Digger character is known for her willingness to use sexuality for financial gain. Tiara's behavior within the episodes also communicates her sexualized nature. In one episode, Tiara brags about the attention she is receiving from a guy who was previously interested in her roommate. During the episode, Tiara laughs with fellow Black cast member Nastasia about a guy's advances toward Tiara. The women have the following verbal exchange while dancing provocatively in a nightclub:

> Nastasia: T, you better take that, bitch!
> Tiara: Bitch, he want it!

Nastasia's statement implied that Tiara should take control ("take that, bitch") of the guy who was interested in her. The way in which Tiara responded illustrates how boastful she is about the fact that the guy is attracted to her. The way she delivered the message, while laughing and bragging, also implies her ability to actually "take that." Her demeanor and her dialogue communicate the hypersexual nature of the Sexualized Black Woman.

Another example of the Sexualized Black Woman was presented in *The Real World Cancun* as cast member Jasmine displayed her need for sex and male attention. In one episode, Jasmine showed her frustrations with the lack of sexual attention she received from a guy who she had attempted to pursue. In a flashback she said, "He didn't even want it. I'm like, are you serious?" Because the scene flashes back to an image of the guy rejecting Jasmine's advances in the bedroom, the audience is led to believe that "it" refers to sexual intercourse. One cast member was filmed saying, "Poor Jasmine is sexually frustrated. She can't get any dick." Jasmine's dependency on sex and male attention are both elements of the Sexualized Black Woman.

None of the women in the PB shows was filmed behaving like the Sexualized Black Woman. In two instances, two of the fourteen female cast members made inappropriate jokes that alluded to sex. For example, during her ultrasound, Phaedra from *The Real Housewives of Atlanta* said, "Well he got a little ole wee-wee. Boy you better get the growing." Her comment about her son's penis size alludes to its importance for sexual intercourse. In an episode of *Basketball Wives* during a wine tasting, Jennifer was asked if she likes nuts to which she laughs and responds, "I haven't had any for a while." The reactions of the women involved in the conversation as well as the context helps viewers recognize that "nuts" is a sexual reference to a man's penis, testicles, and/or ejaculate. However, despite these two instances, none of the 14 women in the PB shows was shown acting in a hypersexual or promiscuous manner like the women in the PNB shows.

Defining Physical Attractiveness

As discussed earlier, both the PB and PNB shows featured Black women who were labeled as attractive or who possessed qualities of physical attractiveness. However, differences existed between the two groups in terms of the type of physical attractiveness portrayed and how this beauty was achieved. The women in the PB shows presented a variety of body types and hairstyles, while the women in the PNB shows were shown abiding by Eurocentric beauty standards. For example, in the cast of *Basketball Wives*, Tami, Royce, and Jenn each have long hair. However, cast member, Shaunie features a shorter hairstyle in all of the episodes analyzed. Similarly, in the cast of *The Real Housewives of Atlanta*, two of the five Black cast members, Nene and Kandi, have short hairstyles in all of the episodes analyzed. The other cast members have longer hairstyles. The PB shows also featured more diversity in the body shapes of the Black cast members. For example, in *Love & Hip Hop*, Olivia has a thinner figure while her fellow cast members Emily, Mashonda, and Chrissy feature more curvaceous figures that would not be classified as thin. This diversity in body shapes is also featured in episodes of *The Real Housewives of Atlanta* and *Basketball Wives*.

In the PNB shows, this amount of diversity was not as apparent. All of the women presented in the three docusoaps had long hair. While Jonna from *The Real World Cancun* has her natural shorter hair in some scenes, she was featured in subsequent scenes with longer hair extensions. Of the six Black cast members across the PNB shows, all but one (Nastasia from *Bad Girls Club*) have thin figures. In two instances, cast members are criticized for not having curvaceous bodies. For example, in an episode of *Bad Girls Club: New Orleans*, Tiara is mocked for having a smaller butt than her non-Black cast member. While arguing over a guy's attention, Tiara and her non-Black roommate Tasha engage in a physical altercation. Afterwards, Tiara accuses her roommate of "wanting to be Black." Her roommate responded:

Tasha:	Wanna be Black? Bitch my ass is bigger than your ass! Come on, let's compare! Let's compare asses! My ass is bigger!
Nastasia:	You got a fat ass boo *(Speaking to Tiara)*.
Tiara:	I got a donkey bitch, don't get it twisted.

Tiara took the comments offensively and responded by standing on her roommate's bed, bending over, and declaring how she has a "donkey." In this context, the connotative meaning of "donkey" is a large butt. A non-African

American cast member is teasing Tasha for not having the big butt expected of Black women. In an episode of *Khloe & Lamar*, Malika is teased (in a lighter manner) for not having a large butt by an Armenian male cast member. While discussing Malika's career aspirations, a male cast member tells her, "If everything fails, I promise you, Miami, Atlanta, they have a great calling for you in the strip club industry. Like you're a pretty girl, but you don't have like that big ATL booty." She responded by jokingly asking if that's all she's missing. In these two examples, Malika and Tiara are described as having small butts. They are mocked because a larger butt is expected of Black women. Their small butts and thin frames align more with Eurocentric beauty standards rather than those for Black women.

The Black women in the PNB shows also reinforced Eurocentric beauty standards through their beauty rituals. For example, Judi, Tiara, and Nastasia from *Bad Girls Club: New Orleans* were often shown putting on make-up. All three women were also shown visiting the hairdresser, during which time Tiara and Nastasia received hair extensions. Tiara expressed how her hair extensions made her more attractive. After her hair appointment, she explained, "My hair looks amazing. I feel like a new person. Like whoever knows me knows that I take my hair very serious." Her description of her hair and how it makes her a "new person" implies that the hair extensions transformed her into another person—one that she considers to be attractive.

Good Bitch, Bad Bitch

In all 20 of the docusoaps, a Black woman was labeled as a bitch by herself or another cast member. The way in which the term was used depended on the context. A Black woman was labeled a bitch in a derogatory fashion when she was engaged in a conflict. For example, Judi from *Bad Girls Club: New Orleans* was called a bitch on several occasions when arguing with a fellow cast member. In one instance, a cast member described Judi's behaviors saying, "The bitch is acting a damn fool. Judi has no respect for herself or others. I'm really tired of dealing with her stupidity." However, a Black woman was also labeled a bitch by a friend as a term of endearment. Judi was also called a bitch by her friends. When the label was assigned by her friends, she laughed and responded positively. In one episode, Nastasia and Judi are featured using the term positively to identify themselves:

Nastasia:	I'm the baddest bitch in the house. I'm the strongest bitch in this house.
Judi:	No, I think I'm the strongest bitch…

To add insult to the term, Black women were also labeled as a bitch with an adjective preceding the word to further explain a character trait or specific moment. For example, in *The Real Housewives of Atlanta,* Nene is told, "You're a dumb bitch." In an episode of *Love & Hip Hop* Chrissy's boyfriend's mother tells her, "You're a selfish bitch. That's how I feel." During an episode of *Basketball Wives*, Tami is described as being a "bum bitch." When the term was used in such an aggressive or demeaning way, the women rejected the label. For example, Nene, from *The Real Housewives of Atlanta,* and Nastasia, from *Bad Girls Club: New Orleans,* both threatened bodily harm in some fashion after being called a bitch during an argument. In another example, Malika from *Khloe & Lamar* defended herself after being called a bitch:

Robert:	No offense, but you're like Khloe's little bitch.
Malika:	I am not Khloe's bitch. Get out of here.

When the term was used to label the Black women in the PB shows it was most often (78%) used in a derogatory fashion. For the PNB women who were labeled as bitches, it was used as a term of endearment more often (64%) than a derogatory term.

· 4 ·

RECLAIMING SEXUALITY

"You know how milk does a body good? But sex does a body good too. And if anything better, God would have kept it to himself."

—GENEVA'S MOTHER, *blood, sweat, and heels*

With prevalent images like the Jezebel and Sexualized Bitch, audiences may be accustomed to a negative portrayal of Black female sexuality. In the majority of instances when in the 2011 study, the female was the minority cast member and her sexuality was framed in a less flattering light. Sex was not a theme that dominated the majority of the docusoaps' storylines in the 2014 analysis. This alone helps communicate the message that Black women are not consumed with sex. However, sex was also not a taboo topic. In the cases where the women's sex lives were discussed, sex was generally not framed in a negative light. This has the potential to help broaden people's views on Black women as sexual beings.

Take, for example, the quote above, which is from a scene of *Blood, Sweat, and Heels*. During a video call, Geneva gets advice from her mother, who is also a sex therapist. Her mother is trying to convince her to pleasure herself since Geneva is not currently in a relationship. She admits that her mom's constant discussion of sex can sometimes be embarrassing. Yet, this embarrassment seems to be attached less to the idea of sex and more to the fact she is discussing her sex life with a parent. In a different scene while attending the Polo Classic, Geneva mimics riding a horse and explains how the event gets her "hot and heavy." She explains how this could be because of her lack of sex and then discusses her need for a vibrator. Her open expression, at this point, shows she is not embarrassed by her sexuality. Although it was quite an uncomfortable experience, Geneva gains *motherly* advice about the need for sex. A parent, who is expected to show concern for her child's well-being, finds sex important and natural enough that it needs to be discussed.

No Shame, Just Girl Talk

Geneva's exchange with her mother is one of several examples where sex is discussed among Black women. Within the same docusoap (*Blood, Sweat, and Heels*) Melyssa proudly talks about her vibrator when it is found by fellow cast member, Daisy. She brags about how effective the product is in helping her quickly reach her sexual climax. In *Married to Medicine*, during a slumber party, Simone, Quad, and Lisa have a discussion about their sex lives with their husbands. The conversation turns to the idea of sexually pleasing your man. After Simone shares that she has never put on a performance for her husband (which is implied as a form of foreplay), Quad inquires more.

> Quad: Don't you want to blow [your husband's] mind?
> Simone: I don't want to blow anything, Quad. I'm not a blower.
> Quad: Well that's a problem.

This exchange illustrates how Quad and Simone are not ashamed to discuss their sex preferences. Simone, who admits to being conservative in the bedroom, finds the conversation with her friends to be informative. During a confessional scene, she explains how the conversation opened her eyes and made her realize that she needed to spice up her and her husband's intimate life. The women are not vulgar in their exchange, but freely discuss sexual activities. For some, this may show their appropriateness in discussing their sex lives.

The ladies of *SWV Reunited* also have candid girl talks about their sex lives. However, on this particular docusoap the women focus a lot of attention on one cast member—Lelee. Taj refers to Lelee as a little freak, although not in an insulting manner. Coko refers to Lelee as a "trysexual" because of her experimental nature in the bedroom. In fact, both Taj and Coko discuss how

Lelee taught them everything about sex. The women's discussions were often full of laughter. Although they playfully teased Lelee, they did not seriously shame her for her actions.

Lelee was very open about her sexuality. She owned it. In one episode, the ladies are discussing their sex lives. Coko playfully calls Lelee a "ho" and a "humper" before asking about her number of sexual partners. Coko suggests the number 20 and Lelee nonchalantly replies, "Maybe." She is also shown in other scenes celebrating her sexuality such as when she visits the plastic surgeon and moves her butt in a circular motion while being examined by the doctor. She also talks about her crush on President Barack Obama and the excitement that she imagines would come from getting some "White House ass." Some may identify Lelee's behaviors as hypersexual; however, she has no shame about her actions. She does, however, try to put less focus on sex in other scenarios in the series and has a broader character development and "arc" than just a sexual being.

Friends Kalenna and Rasheedah from *Love & Hip Hop Atlanta* discuss Kalenna's nontraditional relationship with her husband, Tony and her friend, Ashley. Kalenna admits to being bisexual and having sexual encounters with both of them. She shamelessly discusses threesomes. When Ashley leaves after a recent visit, Rasheedah and Kalenna talk about the situation. Kalenna decided that it was time to cool things off with Ashley and focus on her home, husband, and career. She also reveals that she is pregnant. But, when asked, Kalenna does confirm that she and Ashley did get physical during her recent visit.

> Rasheedah: You ole bisexual freaky ass bitch. I can't deal.
> Kalenna: You better know it.

The two laugh and high five, which shows viewers that the exchange was all in fun. There was no negative judgment or shame attached. To some, Kalenna's sex life may be far from ordinary. In fact, some may consider it to be unacceptable. Yet, the assessment of her behavior is up to the audience members. The women in the show do not explicitly label her actions as being negative. Instead, they seem acceptable.

Within some examples of girl talk, the women played games that discuss sex. During Kandi's bachelorette party on *Kandi's Wedding*, sex was a dominant theme. As the women celebrated, they passed around penis-shaped toys while being entertained by female strippers (a plus-size stripper and a little-person stripper). Younger and older women enjoyed the festivities. This display of sex seemed to be all in good fun. Such practices are common at bachelorette parties, so the women were engaging in a type of fun that some may consider appropriate to the occasion.

On an episode of *Hollywood Exes* during a game of truth or dare, Nicole accepted a dare to use a piece of celery covered with peanut butter to demonstrate how she performs oral sex on her fiancé. The women laughed and joked throughout the activity, including pastor's wife Sheree. The women were also shown playing a game of "Marry, Screw, Kill" in which the women had to explain who they would marry, have sex with, or murder out of a list of three people. The ladies on *SWV Reunited* were also filmed playing this game. Some audience members may argue that it hints to the women's sexualized nature. However, the way in which the women engaged in the activities showed that they considered them appropriate during their playful discussion about sex. Furthermore, others may argue that their willingness to play a game does not translate to promiscuity.

Sex and Relationships

One of the characteristics of the traditional hypersexual Black woman is that she was overly and irresponsibly sexual. According to the stereotypes, her careless attitude toward sex warranted rape from slave masters. In more recent images such as the Baby Momma, her irresponsible actions result in multiple children. Gray's (2009) analysis of dating shows revealed how women's sexuality was only used to gain a man's attention. But sexuality in several docusoaps was presented in a somewhat different light. For example, many discussions about sex are about women within relationships. The majority of the women are not discussing casual sex with multiple partners. In fact, many of them are married. For some, this may make their discussions of sex more appropriate. Although they may have been using sexuality to get a man's attention, in most cases it was their spouse or significant other—not a random guy.

Let's look at the slumber party chat with Simone, Quad, and Lisa from *Married to Medicine*. Each of the women is discussing their sexual activities with their husbands. The ladies also have conversations about sex in a mixed group during their couples' retreat. One night during the trip, the couples sit roundtable style and discuss how often married couples should have sex. Toya and her husband Eugene state that time constraints made it difficult for them to have sex as often as they wanted to.

In an episode of *Marriage Boot Camp*, sex is one theme of a therapy session, further illustrating that it is a natural part of marriages. Gloria and Tasha's spouses say that they wish to have more sex within their relationships. Gloria feels that her husband is too focused on sex while she is focused on emotions and romance. In front of the other couples, Tasha expresses anger that her husband keeps saying she does not like sex. She even mentions how she enjoys oral sex and being thrown on the table. She also tells him, "I've got whips. I've got collars. I've got outfits. I've got costumes. I've got oil, creams, and lotions." At one point, both Gloria and Tasha have sex with their husbands at Marriage Boot Camp. This behavior is completely opposite of that of the stereotypical hypersexual Black woman. The women do enjoy sex but they are not over-sexualized—in fact, their husbands request more sex. So what is commonly portrayed is their sexual intercourse takes place within the context of their committed relationships.

Married couples Erica and Warren Campbell (*Mary Mary*) and Cynthia and Peter Thomas (*The Real Housewives of Atlanta*) have flirtatious moments and conversations that allude to their sex lives. Traci and her husband Kevin (*Marriage Boot Camp: Reality Stars*) have a little chuckle when the other houseguests say they "heard them last night." Although the houseguests mean snoring, for a minute Traci thinks they meant sex. Kevin also mentions the great make-up sex they had after a fight, furthering admitting that they had sex in the Boot Camp house. In the same docusoap, Tanisha expresses her sexual desire for her husband saying, "I so wanna do you right now." Each of these examples shows the women as sexual beings in relation to their spouses. Instead of simple promiscuity, many of the women are discussing (or engaging in) sex in regard to their own relationships.

Of course sex was not reserved for married couples within the docusoaps, which some may argue is an accurate representation of the real world. Draya from *Basketball Wives LA* is in a new committed relationship. Viewers watch as she celebrates a 6-month anniversary with her boyfriend, Orlando. During girl time with Malaysia and Brandi, Draya discusses her relationship with Orlando and explains how she is so proud of herself and feels like a grown woman because they are using condoms. When Slim's boyfriend comes over to visit on *Bad Girls Club: Chicago*, the two have sex. Instead of criticizing her, Blu says, "I'm glad somebody around this house getting some action." Not only is it okay that Slim is having sex, Blu's comment implies that other women wished they were getting that *action*.

Kandi from *The Real Housewives of Atlanta* makes references to her sex life with her fiancé, Todd. During a spa day when Porsha jokes about the size of Kandi's butt and Todd having to "climb all of that," Kandi explains how he is able to do so because of his "pole," alluding to his penis size. Not only are Kandi and Todd in a committed relationship, viewers see their road to marriage in a different docusoap, *Kandi's Wedding*. During that series, Kandi still discusses her sex life. At the end of her bachelorette party Kandi says, "So we didn't see any dick tonight, but I still had a great time. And now I'm ready to get married to my life long dick at home."

Followers of Kandi's career are probably not surprised by her choice of language and views toward sex. After all, she does own a sex toy line and hosts a sex-themed online talk show called *Kandi Koated Nights*. Her word choice is far from conservative, and Kandi's comment shows how she is not embarrassed about her sexual desires. She is also not reprimanded or shamed by her friends. Lastly, she is referring to sexual relations within her committed relationship and not to promiscuous and random booty calls.

In *Love & Hip Hop Atlanta*, Mimi's sex tape with her boyfriend Nikko was a constant topic of conversation. However, prior to the release of her sex tape, Mimi and her friends candidly talked about their sex lives. The women's exchange indicated that it was okay for Mimi to engage in sexual relations with her significant other—even if not in the traditional manner. The later criticism was sparked by the fact that Mimi's private sex tape was eventually released to the public. Several members of the cast expressed their disgust with her decision. According to Mimi and Nikko, the sex tape was leaked to the public after it was stolen. While traveling, Nikko lost his luggage, which included the video camera and footage. Mimi appears devastated when this is brought to her attention.

After constant urging by Nikko, Mimi agrees to accept a pornography company's request to professionally edit and release the tape. Many criticize her decision, including the father of her child. He feels it is inappropriate that, as a mother, she has a sex tape. Her friend Erica echoes this sentiment. In fact, during a confessional scene, Erica says that she is heartbroken over Mimi's sex tape. As a mother herself, Erica feels that it was inappropriate and especially damaging to Mimi's daughter. She admits to Mimi that she does not really think that the tape began as a home video just for the couple's private enjoyment. However, Mimi continues to defend her decision. Ultimately it appears that the issue is not Mimi's sexual activities with her boyfriend but, rather, the fact that those private moments became public. Some viewers may also consider Mimi's public sex tape to be inappropriate.

She's a Ho

In most instances, women's sexuality was discussed and framed by the women in a positive light. However, there were a few instances when a woman criticized another woman's sex life. Although the term "ho" was used playfully in *SWV Reunited*, the label was used as an insult in the docusoap *Basketball Wives LA*. At different points throughout the docusoap, Draya's past and sexuality are discussed by other cast members. Fellow cast members bring up her bisexuality, history as a stripper, and previous sexual encounters. During their first meeting as a group, Brittish asks Draya, "Are you a ho for real?" Draya denies this and is visibly offended. In a different episode Sundy characterizes Draya based on what she perceives to be her sexual nature: "Girls like Draya show up, to me, at hotels. They figure out where this person's gonna be and they kind of target these men." Although Sundy criticizes Draya, Sundy's own sexual habits are criticized. During an argument, Brandi screams to Sundy that her "pussy is disgusting" and calls her a tramp and a ho for having a child by a married man. As they argue, Sundy also calls Brandi a ho.

Phaedra, from *The Real Housewives of Atlanta*, refers to Kenya as a ho on more than one occasion. In one episode she renames her castmate, "Kenya Moore Whore" because of her inappropriate actions towards Phaedra's husband. During an activity on *Marriage Boot Camp*, Gloria's husband feels she is flirting with another man. He becomes very upset and calls her a ho. The activity is the first time Gloria has met the other man and their encounter is recorded for the other housemates to see. Although she is not shown engaging in sexual intercourse with the other man, her husband uses the word as an insult for what he perceives to be inappropriate behavior. In each of these instances, a Black woman's sexual behaviors are criticized when they are considered inappropriate. In an episode of *Love & Hip Hop Atlanta*, the term "ho" is used as an insult in response to infidelity. It was sparked by the following exchange:

> Karlie: I'm just asking you are you fuckin' my man or not.
> Khadiyah: I absolutely am. Every night.

The smirk on Khadiyah's face shows that she is unashamed of her behaviors. It also appears that she was aware Joc (the man being discussed) was in a relationship with Karlie. She did not deny Karlie's declaration that he was *her* man. Following a physical altercation, Karlie calls Khadiyah (and Joc) a ho. Again, the term is used as an insult. The fact that the term is used sometimes as an insult and ammunition in a conflict, communicates that such behavior (acting as a ho) is regarded as bad.

In episodes of *Marriage Boot Camp: Reality Stars*, Tanisha and Traci admit to their infidelity. Audience members may assume that this infidelity includes sex with someone outside of the marriage. Both ladies argue that their spouses cheated on them first. During a therapy session Traci explained that she cheated on her husband in order to make him hurt (as she did) and because she wanted to feel beautiful and special. To some, it may come off that the women were trying to justify their behaviors. While the counselors and spouses express how the infidelity is wrong, it was done so in a way where the women were not constantly shamed or labeled for their behaviors.

Overall, Black women's sexuality was a topic discussed within many of the docusoaps. Whether during girl talk, playful games, or when communicating with the opposite sex, the women do not have a problem talking about their sexual desires. There were some examples where a woman's sexual nature is explicitly labeled as negative and inappropriate. Most times, this insult was delivered in the midst of an argument—similar to the PNB shows in the 2011 analysis. In other instances, the women's sexual behavior is not criticized, and the audience is left to draw their own conclusion. A positive is that there is improvement in terms of media representations of Black women's sexuality insomuch as audiences are provided with alternative portrayals than just exclusively negative portrayals. In addition the women were not shown as only engaging in or discussing sexual activities, which were treated as only one element of their characters.

· 5 ·

BLACK MOTHERHOOD

"I may not be the best mom but can't nobody say I didn't try."
— Momma Joyce, *Kandi's Wedding*.

Even within docusoaps in which the women were not mothers (e.g. *Bad Girls Club: Chicago* and *Blood, Sweat, and Heels*), the importance of a mother figure is communicated in some of the women's interactions. This theme was more apparent in the 2014 analysis than in the 2011 analysis. Geneva is shown video chatting with her mom while they discuss relationships and her career. Her mother offers advice and guidance. In a different episode, Geneva's mother convinces her to attend a dinner with the other women that was being held to relieve existing tensions. Daisy's mother comes to support her daughter at her business event. During family day on *Bad Girls Club: Chicago*, Blu was very excited that her mother was one of the guests who came to visit. The two appear to have a close relationship. Although the main cast does not include mothers, the influence and supportive nature of motherhood are exhibited.

The joy of motherhood is inherent in several of the women's stories—even in the planning for motherhood. Brandi from *Basketball Wives LA* chronicles her attempts to have another child. Unfortunately it has not been an easy task because of her medical history, which includes cancer. Her determination to visit fertility doctors and prayers for another child illustrate how much she cherishes the role. Jackie from *Married to Medicine* faces a similar dilemma. Although she desperately wants to have a baby, she is unable to do so because of her past battle with cancer. On multiple occasions Jackie discusses her desire to have children—even if that requires adoption. When conversing with her office manager and one of her patients, Jackie discusses how women feel they are born to be mothers and sometimes feel guilty as she does when she can't give her husband a son. Jackie's comments and experiences indicate the value of motherhood and her belief that being a mother is part of her duty as a woman.

Mommy: More Than Just a Title

In the majority of the docusoaps in which at least one Black cast member is a mother, we see examples of the women interacting with their children. In *Marrying the Game*, Tiffney is shown engaging in several activities with her son and daughter including reading a bedtime story, painting pottery, decorating cakes, and hanging out at home. Heavenly from *Married to Medicine* creates a vision board with her daughter and talks to her about her goals and aspirations. Taj from *SWV Reunited* plays basketball outside with her son and husband. Kandi's daughter, Riley, accompanies her during some of her wedding preparations on *Kandi's Wedding*. Such interactions were not reserved for younger children. Kim, a 40+ year old Black woman in *L.A. Hair* is shown interacting with her mother, Jas, inside and outside of her hair salon.

The women's different interactions show how being a mom is more than just a label. Unlike the stereotypical characterization of the careless Baby Momma or Welfare Momma, many of the Black mothers across the docusoaps demonstrate care, concern, support, and protection for their children. Tiffney from *Marrying the Game* takes her daughter Cali to a casting director after Cali expresses an interest in acting. Tiffney also meets with a more seasoned "momager" (Sonya Norwood) to get advice on her daughter entering show business at such a young age. Not only does Tiffney invest time into her daughter's dream but she researches the consequences of such a decision.

When facing dilemmas, some of the mothers' first concern was for their children. While playing soccer with her son in the park, Draya talks to him about how excited she is that he is finally living with her. She explains that it was always her goal and that it only took some time because she had to make sure she had things in order. She then asks her son how he feels about her current relationship. She proudly boasts about the fact that her current boyfriend gets along with her son. It is one of the things she enjoys about her new relationship.

Tiffney (*Marrying the Game*) also faces concerns about the impact of a romantic relationship on her children; however, her situation is much different. She and her fiancé (who is also the father of her children) decide to end their relationship. In the season of the docusoap that was analyzed, the children are now living with their mom and dad in separate homes. On different occasions Tiffney explains how she is heartbroken for her children who have to go through such a transition. She is so worried about her children's experience that it motivates her to write a children's book to help young children deal with divorce and separation.

Care and concern for your children should be a factor in your decisions. This is a point that was stressed in *Love & Hip Hop Atlanta* when cast members discussed Mimi's sex tape. Mimi explains how she is overwhelmed by people's responses to the sex tape. She is especially bothered by the comments about her being an unfit mother because of her decision. Even her friend Erica D., a mother herself, was upset about the decision to release the sex tape because of the impact it would have on Mimi's daughter. Mimi defended her actions and said that she did think about the future of her family, which includes her daughter. Here, we see that concern is expected, even from outsiders looking in. To accuse a mother of not providing sufficient care is seen as an insult.

In some cases, the way in which a Black mother demonstrated her concern and protection was unconventional or not necessarily seen as positive. Kandi and her mother, Momma Joyce, are featured in two docusoaps—*The Real Housewives of Atlanta* and *Kandi's Wedding*. In both shows, one of the common storylines deals with Momma Joyce's disapproval of Kandi's decision to marry her fiancé, Todd. As Momma Joyce explains to her sisters (Aunt Bertha and Aunt Nora), she does not dislike Todd, but just feels that he does not have Kandi's best interests in mind. Momma Joyce gets into multiple disagreements with people about this topic including Todd, his mother Sharon, and Kandi's friend and assistant, Carmon. However, as the opening quote illustrates, Momma Joyce felt that she was fulfilling her role as a good mother. Her actions were her way of protecting her daughter's well-being.

Some people criticize Momma Joyce for her methods. Thus, her presentation could be viewed in more than one way. Some may see her desire to protect Kandi as too aggressive and inappropriate, while others may consider her actions to be signs of a mother's love. It is up to the audience members' own interpretation. The same could be the case for Rasheedah's mother (*Love & Hip Hop Atlanta*). In one episode, Rasheedah discusses the tension between her husband, Kirk, and her mother. She refers to the time when her mother ran over Kirk's bike to punish him for his infidelities. Again, a mother took drastic measures to protect and defend her daughter. To Rasheedah, it was more understandable; to Kirk, it was too extreme.

The same could be argued about Gloria's reaction in an episode of *Marriage Boot Camp*. Each of the couples is given an opportunity to ask their spouse a question during a lie detector test. Gloria decided to use the opportunity to ask her husband if he loved their birth children more than his stepson (her biological child). Her husband responded, "yes" on the test, and it was revealed that he was telling the truth. Gloria becomes very upset at his revelation. This is yet another situation where viewers may differ as to whether they believe Gloria's behavior is that of a protective mother or that of an overly aggressive woman.

Baby Momma versus Mother of Their Child

When meeting with Jackie for the first time on *Basketball Wives LA*, Ariane makes it very clear that she is the mother of her ex's children; she is not a Baby Momma. Making this distinction is understandable considering the negative connotation attached to the term "Baby Momma." Many of the shows have names that suggest relationships and family—*Basketball **Wives***, *Real **Housewives*** *of Atlanta*, and *Kandi's **Wedding***. Even though many of the women in the shows are no longer in relationships with the father of their children, the titles of the shows center on relationships.

The women's mothering skills and interactions with their children also frame them as better mothers than the stereotypical Baby Momma. Furthermore, some of the mothers (e.g., Taj and Coko from *SWV Reunited*) are still married to the father of their children. At the time of filming, Jackie, Malaysia, and Brandi from *Basketball Wives LA* were also married to their children's father. Although dealing with marital issues during the series, Tina from *Mary Mary* was still married to her children's father as was her sister Erica. Rasheedah and her husband were also shown reconciling and taking care of their new son.

The stereotypical Baby Momma is also accused of harassing her children's father for money. Oftentimes she uses that money for her own purposes. The women of *Hollywood Exes* shine light specifically on the need for financial assistance and how the media and public often perceive it in a negative light. During a dinner party with all of the women, Andrea gets very upset with Mayte who makes a comment about her experiences as a mother being different than Sheree's experiences because Sheree has "Will Smith money." Andrea quickly defends Sheree while explaining that the media always portray the former wives of celebrities as being money hungry and frivolously asking for their celebrity exes' financial support.

In a later scene, Andrea and Mayte sit down to have a calmer exchange. Andrea explains how difficult it is to get assistance from the father of her children and that it is frustrating because the money is used to support her kids and not herself. Andrea's comments and the women's discussions help make a distinction between the irresponsible mother who misuses financial support and the devoted mother who requires child support only to take proper care of her children.

Professional Moms

Stereotypical portrayals of the working mother (e.g., the Matriarch) characterized Black women as being unable to balance both motherhood and professional careers. Several of the Black women had careers outside of the home. In fact, the majority of the women were shown more often in their professional lives than in the domestic realm historically reserved for mothers. Although Fairclough's (2004) analysis of lifestyle reality shows found that the women's careers were presented as a detriment to their home and parenting skills, this was not the case for our 2014 analysis. In our 2011 analysis, when the Black women were discussed as mothers their careers were also highlighted. However, although this tendency was more prevalent in the cast biographies in the 2011 shows, the 2014 presentations focused more on the women as mothers.

When they have to go on the road, Tina and Erica (*Mary Mary*) have a difficult time leaving their children. They also had their children present at some of their events. Their dual roles—as mothers and artists—also motivate some of their decisions. For example, Tina is hesitant to agree to a concert in Australia because she does not want to leave her home (husband and children) for ten days. She does not make a decision until she speaks with her children. The sisters and their manager attend a branding meeting to discuss a new *Mary Mary* handbag. Tina explains how she and Erica want to make a product for mothers and their children.

Marrying the Game's Tiffney is the mother of two and a schoolteacher. She is portrayed as a nurturing woman at home with her children and in the classroom with her students. When she decides to write a book to help with her healing process (dealing with the break-up), she chooses her topic based on her own children's experiences. Her professional endeavor is guided by her experiences as a mother and her concern for her son and daughter as they deal with their parents' separation.

Coko also makes a career decision based on her role as a mother. At the last minute she informs her group members, Taj and Lelee, that she will not be able to perform at a scheduled concert. Instead she needs to be home with her son, who has an upcoming court appearance. Although Taj and Lelee are extremely upset with Coko's decision they later explain that they understand her position as a mother and were only upset at the last-minute cancellation and lack of communication. Here, the Black woman was a professional mom, but her children were more important than her career.

Although some of the mothers are able to work and raise children, Simone (*Married to Medicine*) makes it clear that it is not always an easy task. She is a gynecologist and the mother of two children. Her friend and fellow doctor Jackie expresses her desire for children. To help her understand how difficult it can be, Simone presents Jackie with a baby doll that reacts like a real child. Jackie quickly says that she is up for the tasks and boasts that she will work and keep the baby from crying. In a subsequent scene, Jackie gets into her car after a long, late night of delivering babies. She speaks directly to the camera and explains that on nights like that particular one, she does not know what she would do if she had a baby of her own. She then turns around, realizes the baby doll is in the back seat, and acknowledges that she forgot all about the mechanical child.

Quad (*Married to Medicine*) also recognizes the time commitment associated with being a mother. She and her husband, Greg, have what appears to be an ongoing decision process about his desire for children and her decision to wait until her puppy couture clothing line is up and running. Greg feels that Quad does not respect his desire for a child. She explains that it is important for her to first gain economic independence and to see what she can do as a business owner. Some may view Quad's decision as selfish. During couples' group chat, Toya's husband, Eugene, explains that when couples get married, they both take ownership of the money and the uterus. He believes that a woman should not decide on her own that she does not want to have children. But Quad's decision to not have children at this time also helps to debunk the stereotype of the irresponsible Black mother. She is both honest and upfront about her desires. Instead of having a child carelessly and then intentionally devoting more attention to her career than her son and daughter, Quad chooses to wait to have children.

Whether working moms or women contemplating motherhood, the different images communicate how Black women are capable of raising their children and working outside of the home. Yet the experiences of Quad and Jackie also shine light on the reality that working and raising children is not an easy task. The variety in images also acknowledges that all Black women are not on one side of the debate—to have children or not to have children.

Moms with Status

Of course, we have to acknowledge the socioeconomic status of these women and the role socioeconomic status plays in mothering. For example, as mentioned before, Tiffney takes her daughter Cali to visit a casting director. The average mother does not have access to such opportunities. We can assume that Tiffney's status and connections in the industry made it possible for her (and her daughter) to meet with a casting director.

All mothers are not able to bring their children to work, like mothers Tina and Erica (*Mary Mary*) do. These recording artists, like Coko and Taj (*SWV Reunited*), often have to leave their homes and children to go on the road. They have access to childcare—whether it is outside services or family members who can afford to stay home without working—that helps them to fulfill their roles as both mothers and professionals. This is not to criticize the women for their access to such resources. However, we would be remiss if we did not acknowledge the role their status plays in their ability to juggle motherhood and professional lives. The fact remains that many women who do not have the same resources as these women are still able to raise their children and handle a career, though this is far from an easy task.

Parenting Troubles

We also see examples of the issues that Black women had with their children. Both Jackie and Sundy from *Basketball Wives LA* discussed troubling relationships with their daughters. Flashbacks to the previous season show the issues Jackie is having with her daughter Chantel. During a therapy session, Chantel explains that she and her sister are angry with their mother, Jackie. In a confessional,

Jackie explains that her relationship with Chantel was still rocky but improving. We see Jackie and Chantel interacting, which allowed the audience (especially fans and avid viewers of the show) to see some of the improvement.

Sundy confides in Jackie about the issues she is having with her daughter. Her daughter called her a whore, so we can infer that their relationship is hostile. Now Sundy is dealing with an Internet rumor that she posted a photo of her daughter in a compromising position that implied she was performing oral sex on a man. Sundy explains how it is a very emotional experience dealing with the rumors, critiques of her parenting, and the fact that she and her daughter are not on speaking terms. Later, in a different episode, Sundy is interacting with her other daughter and son. She discusses her desire to rebuild the relationship with her daughter and wants to make it clear to her children that she will always be there for them.

Coko's son (*SWV Reunited*) is facing legal issues in their hometown. As the court date approaches, Coko becomes increasingly concerned about whether her son will show up. She reveals that her son left home and cut off all contact with her. He does eventually arrive for court and attends with his mom and family by his side. But Coko blames herself for her son's behavior. She wonders if her time away from home while she was on the road impacted his decisions. Part of the Black Matriarch's negative image is that her children's failures are her fault. Coko's concerns align with this image.

When visiting Coko after her son's court date, Lelee shares that her son had legal issues and had to serve time in jail. Yet instead of taking ownership of her son's problems she maintains that jail helped set her son on the right path. It took getting into trouble for him to realize that his decisions were destructive. The juxtaposition of Coko's experience with Lelee's helps present a multidimensional view. The stereotypical Matriarch is undoubtedly at fault for her children's misfortunes. However, in the docusoap the show does not frame the women's career choices as the reason for their children's troubles. Instead, the Black mothers themselves present two views of the same issue—it is my fault versus it is not my fault.

Lelee also discusses some issues that she is having with her children. Being a single mother for the majority of her son's and daughters' lives, the three of them have been in the same household for several years. Yet she vents to her friends and groupmates (Coko and Taj) about how her children are at the age when it is time for them to move out. Lelee's parenting issue also communicates the idea that as a mother, it is not her responsibility to care for her children forever.

· 6 ·

PHYSICAL APPEARANCE

"Honey, Ms. Quad's body is snatched. You can't buy this in the store, honey. Sorry, Heavenly [and] Mariah."

— QUAD, *MARRIED TO MEDICINE*

Like the 2011 analysis, the 2014 season of the docusoaps featured Black women with various complexions, body contours, and hairstyles. All of the women on the show do not meet the Eurocentric body standards that have long been reinforced in media representations. *The Real Housewives of Atlanta*, for example, features Kandi, who is a shorter woman with a more curvaceous body type. On the same docusoap viewers see Cynthia, a taller woman with a more slender frame. On *Blood, Sweat, and Heels* Melyssa and Brie have lighter skin tones while Geneva and Daisy present darker skin tones. On *L.A. Hair*, Kim and her mother Jas have darker skin tones. China, on the other hand, has a lighter skin tone. During an episode of this docusoap, viewers also watch Kim prepare for a photo shoot for a book project about the beauty of dark skin tones.

Body Styles: From Skinny to Voluptuous

According to Eurocentric beauty standards, a thin body is attractive. This was not the only body type featured on the docusoaps. Kenya from *The Real Housewives of Atlanta* calls Nene "skinny mini" during one of their encounters. Although Nene has a curvaceous body, her cast member acknowledges that she is not overweight. Her comment does, however, continue to communicate the message that being called skinny is a compliment. During episodes of *Kandi's Wedding*, Momma Joyce also communicates the reverse; that being called fat is an insult. She criticizes Kandi's recent weight gain and tells her daughter that she needs to work on the size of her butt. Being fat is also used as an insult following an altercation on *Basketball Wives*. Draya and Brittish have a disagreement during their first formal meeting. When Draya meets with her friend Malaysia to discuss the incident, she refers to Brittish as "the chubby girl." The way she uses this description while also discussing a conflict, makes the label an insult. The same is true in an episode of *Love & Hip Hop Atlanta* when Karlie is involved in a conflict with a Black woman who has a heavier body type than her own. As an insult, she refers to the woman as a "Teletubby."

The ladies from *SWV Reunited* also discuss how being called fat is an insult. Lelee and Coko both have elective plastic surgery. The women have liposuction and Lelee also has a Brazilian butt lift. When justifying her decision, Coko explains how it is difficult being fat in a singing group. Lelee echoes her thoughts and says that they are in an industry competing with much younger girls. On stage, Lelee jokes about their plastic surgery, saying it was because they were tired of the fans calling them fat.

Demetria (*Blood, Sweat, and Heels*) is dealing with body image issues during her book cover photo shoot. She wishes she did not have to be on the cover and implies that she is uncomfortable with her weight. After explaining that she went on a liquid diet leading up to the shoot, her intern and friend talked to her about loving herself regardless of her size. Despite the encouragement, Demetria still asks if she should suck in her stomach for the pictures.

Kandi's male hairstylist suggests that she and her business partner rename the plus-size section in their women's clothing boutique. According to the stylist—who also considers himself curvy and wears women's clothing—the term plus size may be unflattering. Collectively they decide on the new name—"For the Curvy Girl." The description embraces a woman's curves and also communicates how curvier is more appealing than fat. There are also instances within the docusoaps where the women playfully celebrate their curves. During a spa day Porsha teases Kandi about the size of her butt. Although Momma Joyce criticizes Kandi's size, it does not appear that Porsha means her comment as an insult. Todd also explains how he noticed, and liked, the size of Kandi's butt when they first met. In a different episode at dance rehearsal, Porsha jokes that she cannot lose her butt, especially since she is single and back on the dating market. Taj (*SWV Reunited*) tells Lelee that her date will love her when he sees her butt. Melyssa from *Blood, Sweat, and Heels* also likes her large butt and proudly declares, "The boys seems to like it. Owww!" Quad even playfully teases Simone for her lack of curves, saying she had "no ass." Redd, from *Bad Girls Club: Chicago*, playfully refers to her large body. She is not ashamed of her body type, as she is shown naked in front of her other housemates (in the shower). She also playfully attempts to put on clothing that belongs to one of her thinner roommates.

The different body types and responses to them help communicate that a woman does not have to be thin in order to be considered attractive. However, a new body shape may be communicated within these docusoap presentations as a new standard of attractiveness. The curvaceous body presented and the comments about female body parts—especially in terms of their butts—may indicate that this is more the ideal body type for Black women. In some instances, being fat (and not curvaceous) is still deemed undesirable. Lastly, the fact that some of the women tie their curvaceous body to male attention also conveys that this body frame is attractive. It also may possibly show that a woman should want this body type in order to garner positive attention from others, especially from men.

Relaxers, Weaves, and Natural Hair

Afrocentric styles, such as afros, are rarely celebrated in media messages. The docusoaps were no exception. However, Demetria's (*Blood, Sweat, and Heels*), Blu's (*Bad Girls Club: Chicago*), China's (*L.A. Hair*) and Gloria's (*Marriage Boot Camp*) hairstyles look similar to an afro and their hair was not negatively critiqued. Kandi (*The Real Housewives of Atlanta* and *Kandi's Wedding*) wears her hair in many hairstyles throughout the docusoaps, one of which is a coarser, curly hairstyle that mimics an afro.

Many of the women wear hair weaves and extensions, and unapologetically so. Porsha (*The Real Housewives of Atlanta*) is shown brushing her hair extensions before putting them on her head. Daisy (*Blood, Sweat, and Heels*) is shown preparing for a date and shifting the wig on her head. Coko (*SWV Reunited*) is walking on the pier with her husband and mentions the physical activity may cause her to sweat out her weave. Kim (*L.A. Hair*) discusses her weave and love for big hair while preparing for a photo shoot. During a couples' activity that required fire on *Marriage Boot Camp: Reality Stars*, Tanisha expressed concern that her weave would catch on fire.

The changes in hairstyles help show that the women are wearing some type of hair extension. A cast member with short hair in one instance may have a completely different hairstyle in a later scene. For example, Nene (*The Real Housewives of Atlanta*) has a short hairstyle while attending Cynthia's grand opening party for her new office space. When the ladies gather together for a spa day, Nene's hair is now longer and in a style that comes above her shoulder but past her ear. In an episode of *L.A. Hair* Angela removes her hair extension while at a restaurant with cast member, Naja. During a previous altercation, Naja refers to Angela as fake and references her fake hair, nails, and eyelashes. Angela begins to unclip and remove her extensions in order to show that her hair does not define her as a person.

On one hand, using hair extensions could be seen as an example of the women adhering to Eurocentric beauty standards. However, the women's different hairstyles—some of which do not meet those beauty standards—could communicate that their choice of hairstyle is made according to their own preferences and self-expression. Viewers see Black women wearing hairstyles that vary in length, texture, and color.

You Are What You Wear

In each of the docusoaps, the women wear a variety of clothing and accessories in different situations—loose clothing and fitted clothing, shirts with cleavage and shirts without cleavage, and dresses that vary in length. Viewers will have to decide how appropriate they consider some of the clothing and determine if the clothing fits the occasion. For example, in one scene the women on *The Real Housewives of Atlanta* are featured wearing lingerie at a couples' party. Although many might consider it inappropriate to wear lingerie outside of your home (or the bedroom with your significant other, for that matter), others may argue that the type of clothing fits the occasion—a themed party. The same case could be argued for Quad (*Married to Medicine*) who shows up to Simone's house in lingerie to attend an all-girls lingerie party.

The women's clothing choices may be evaluated based on their occupation. For example, while at her medical office, Jackie (*Married to Medicine*) is wearing a white coat, mid-length skirt (below knee), and sweater. Her appearance seems to fit the professional setting. In a scene of *Blood, Sweat, and Heels*, Melyssa is also shown in her professional setting as a real estate agent. She is making the transition to this new career after being a video girl for several years. Her boss meets with her and tells her to "lose the heels" and hustle harder. While showing a property to a potential buyer, Melyssa is wearing a fitted dress that accentuates her shape. The male client makes a joke about the size of Melyssa's butt and her appearance in the dress. He then asks if her appearance was one of her sales strategies. She laughs in response.

In a different episode, Demetria comments about Melyssa's profession and appearance: "I definitely admire like, you know, Melyssa's transition from sorta that video girl image. At the same time, I have no idea if Melyssa knows how to make money without using her body or sexuality." If Melyssa did, in fact, wear the dress to help with her sales, she is certainly using her sexuality to her advantage. After all, she did make it clear to friends that guys did like her butt size, as discussed earlier. She also discusses how easy it was for her working in the entertainment industry where she was often paid to attend events, "stand there and look good." In this sense, she treats her appearance as a valuable asset; similar to what Waggoner found in an analysis of competition shows. However, Melyssa never confirmed if her attire was intentionally suggestive. Yet her history as a video girl and her response to the client may lead people to believe her attire was strategic. If so, this does not help to build her reputation as a business professional based on skill alone. This practice also contributes to her objectification as a woman. While physical attractiveness was a dominant theme, using it in this manner was not.

When the women show cleavage or wear tight clothing, some might feel these clothing options contribute to the women's own sexual objectification. Viewers could assume that reality television participants pick their own wardrobe. Unlike fully scripted programming, the cast is not expected to visit a wardrobe department to get their pre-determined clothing for each scene. Thus, it may appear to viewers that the Black women actively made a choice to dress in provocative ways. The positive side is that the women are not always dressed in this way. Viewers see women in a variety of clothing so the idea does not communicate that Black women always dress provocatively. Considering the women's open discussion of their sexuality and the frequently changing hairstyles and make-up, one might also assume that their decision to wear (or not to wear) fitted clothing or show cleavage was just their own desire to express themselves and their own sexuality.

Is She Pretty or Ugly?

As the saying goes, "beauty is in the eye of the beholder." Viewers will decide for themselves whether the wide variety of physical characteristics displayed by the women are considered beautiful or ugly. There were some instances where the women were explicitly labeled as attractive or unattractive; the latter of which was normally done in the midst of a conflict and used as an insult. In some cases, the compliments were self-bestowed.

Cynthia and Nene are shopping for bathing suits for the upcoming couples' trip to Mexico. Nene proudly explains that she only wears two-piece bathing suits because she does not have any stretch marks. The fact that she boasts about this helps communicate she considers it adds to her attractiveness. We can refer to Quad's comment that opens the chapter for another example. Letting the viewers know that her body is "snatched" tells us that she considers herself to be attractive. Her sarcastic apology to Mariah and Heavenly about not being able to purchase that type of body also implies that she is more fortunate than they are when it comes to appearance. Momma Joyce also boasts about her appearance and recent weight loss. During their dress-shopping trip on *Kandi's Wedding* she brags about how good she looks in her dress without the help of any type of beauty aid (e.g., girdle, Botox). In a different episode when her hairstylist compliments her on looking nice, she responds, "every day, Baby." Whether the women's comments are considered arrogance or confidence is up to the audience's interpretations.

Shanna (a white cast member) tells Nicole that she has an "incredible body" on an episode of *Hollywood Exes*. Nicole is also a former model, which further establishes her attractiveness. Gloria (*Marriage Boot Camp*) is flattered when her husband compliments her appearance. After he tells her that she looks beautiful, she gets emotional and mentions how she would like to receive such compliments more often. Erica (*Mary Mary*) also receives a compliment from her husband about her physical appearance. As she meets with her stylist and models the proposed clothing option, her husband flirtatiously discusses how she looks while alluding to sex. Brie is told that she looks good while attending a dinner party with her female friends in an episode of *Blood, Sweat, and Heels*. In an episode of *Basketball Wives LA*, Draya calls Brandi and Malaysia beautiful. Kim, from *L.A. Hair* also receives compliments on her appearance when she arrives at her salon on multiple occasions. The fact that these women all have different physical features (e.g., Kim's larger body type and darker skin tone, Gloria's coarser hairstyle, Brie's lighter skin tone) but still received compliments on their appearance helps communicate the subjective nature of beauty.

But in contrast to the compliments, a few of the women's appearances were criticized. Tan and Carmon from *Kandi's Wedding* have a tense relationship. In one episode they both make comments implying that the other woman is unattractive. As discussed earlier, Quad (*Married to Medicine*) makes fun of Heavenly and Mariah's appearances while giving a compliment to herself. Some of the women on *Basketball Wives LA* also commented negatively on the others' appearance. In addition to Draya mocking Brittish's weight (as discussed earlier), Malaysia calls Jackie ugly and old. Jackie refers to one of Malaysia's outfits in a derogatory way explaining, "She looked like a Mediterranean hooker." Brittish mocks Brandi's attire.

In the midst of a disagreement, Geneva from *Blood, Sweat, and Heels* is called Wesley Snipes. This is meant as an insult as Geneva is compared to Snipes' portrayal of a woman—Noxeeema Jackson—in the film *Too Wong Foo, Thanks for Everything! Julie Newmar*. Compliments, and even the women's confidence in their own appearance, help communicate ideas about physical attractiveness. Mocking the women's appearance and referring to them as ugly reinforce the idea that certain physical characteristics are unappealing.

Overall, the shows communicated the idea that being deemed unattractive by others is an insult even as they also illustrate that beauty is subjective. Although Kandi's mother felt that her full-figured body was unattractive, her friends and her fiancé complimented her body. The shows also help communicate the idea that Eurocentric beauty standards are not the norm for everyone. Again, women were depicted as having various skin tones, hair textures, and body shapes. This is not to say that long hair, heavy makeup, and expensive clothing were not common; in fact, we see such styling throughout the shows. However, the variety of appearances shows an improvement in media presentations of Black women.

· 7 ·

SHE HAS HER OWN (MONEY)

"It's almost like Toya's worried that somebody's gonna steal her money man. Boo, I have a job. I make my own money. Don't want your man."

— SIMONE, *MARRIED TO MEDICINE*

Long gone are the days when women are required to stay at home and rely on their husbands' income. Now, this is not to say that women still may not *choose* this option; and there is nothing wrong with that decision. But, women do have the option to generate their own income, and the Black women across the docusoaps help illustrate this point. Even though domesticity is a quality historically linked to women, this was not a dominant theme across the docusoaps. There were some examples when the women were shown (or discussing) household chores such as cleaning or cooking. For example, on *Married to Medicine*, Heavenly, Toya, and Quad explain how it can be sexy to cook for their husbands. Kandi (*The Real Housewives of Atlanta*) and Brittish (*Basketball Wives LA*) are also shown cooking for their significant others. In both cases it appeared to be by choice. None of the women was were restricted to these roles and domestic chores were not a recurring theme. The fact that these women were not required to stay in the household and cooked by choice helps communicate the message that Black women are not required to operate only within the home and the domestic realm.

Financial Stability

Women's social-economic status was evident by their lifestyles as depicted in the docusoaps. Similar to the High Class Black women in the 2011 shows, the 2014 seasons also presented many Black women as prosperous. For example, Andrea, Shamicka, Nicole, and Sheree of *Hollywood Exes* go with their friends on a trip to Hawaii. Nicole also hosts her friend Andrea's wedding at her large, elaborate home. Taj (*SWV: Reunited*) and Nene (*The Real Housewives of Atlanta*) are shown entertaining in their luxurious homes. Kim (*L.A. Hair*) is shown working in her own hair salon and working with several celebrity clients.

Some of the women on *Married to Medicine* boast about their wealth. Quad and Mariah make reference to the *several* furs they own. Toya brags about the new (large) home that she and her family found. Heavenly finds it interesting that Toya and her husband are renting the home and not purchasing it. The fact that she is trying to poke holes in Toya's story makes a few interesting points about money and its value. The assumption that Toya is pretending to be rich and the fact that Heavenly feels the need to expose her story's inconsistencies show how having money and status is something to brag about.

A conflict on *Basketball Wives LA* also communicated that implying someone was pretending to be wealthy was an insult. During an argument between Brandi and Brittish the women begin to yell and throw insults at each other.

> Brittish: Everybody get this bitch out my house!
> Brandi: This ain't your fucking house, bitch. You rent this muthafucker!

Because of the context, it is clear that Brandi meant her comment about Brittish renting her home to be an insult. Although many average viewers may be renters, for these women home ownership is important. Both instances from *Basketball Wives* and *Married to Medicine* communicate the idea that anything less than having enough money to own a home outright will simply not do. The way in which wealth, or lack thereof, is discussed in instances such as these has the potential to reinforce ideas of materialism.

Financial security may be assumed for the recording artists and performers featured on the shows, such as Erica and Tina (*Mary Mary*), Lelee, Coko, and Taj (*SWV: Reunited*), Kandi (*Kandi's Wedding* and *Real Housewives of Atlanta*), Rasheedah and Karlie (*Love & Hip Hop Atlanta*), and Traci (*Marriage Boot Camp: Reality Stars*). Some titles of the shows also hint at the women's economic well-being. **Basketball** *Wives*, *Married to* **Medicine**, and *Marrying the*

Game link the women to profitable industries—pro basketball, medicine, and the rap industry, respectively.

Even if the titles of the shows do not accurately convey the women's net worth, they could lead audience members to make assumptions. It is also no surprise that the participants on these shows are well paid. It is rumored that Nene made $1 million per episode during season 6 of *The Real Housewives of Atlanta*. Their inclusion on the show provides an income and, thus, a job for the Black women. Yet for many, these reality television shows are not their only source of income. In the few instances where the women mentioned financial troubles, it appeared as if they were still able to live comfortably. Simone from *Married to Medicine* and Melyssa from *Blood, Sweat, and Heels* both discussed having to make some alterations to their lifestyles because of recent downswings in their financial situations. However, both women were shown in their well-appointed homes, in nice clothing, and engaging in activities that require money (e.g., Simone planning a couples' trip and Melyssa attending the Polo Classic).

Check Her Resume

Married to Medicine features three doctors on the cast—Simone and Jackie are both obstetricians and Heavenly is a dentist. The other women earned spots on the show because they were doctor's wives. However, that is not their only claim to fame. Because of her professional experience in the fashion industry, Lisa is shown giving advice to Quad who is attempting to launch a clothing line specializing in "puppy couture." Although some consider Quad's business endeavor to be unimportant, as does her husband Greg, she makes it clear that she is entering into a multi-billion dollar industry. She is shown investing time into the project from looking at fabric to researching designers. In a confessional, she explains that she does not want to be seen only as a doctor's wife. Mariah also discusses how she does not get lost in her husband's (who is a doctor) status, while implying that the other women did. She is shown working on her new business—the Cinnamon Girl Diet Program.

L.A. Hair centers on Kimble Hair Studio and the successful career of Kim Kimble. Not only is Kim shown working with several celebrities, other Black women who appear on the show are featured in their careers. China, Jas, and Angela are also hair stylists. In one episode, Angela is shown having a celebratory event for the opening of her own salon. Leah, Kim's sister, is shown in the role of salon manager.

The ladies of *Blood, Sweat, and Heels* are also shown in their professional lives. The title of the show is a play on the quote "Blood, Sweat, and Tears" which refers to the strenuous effort a person puts into a task and implies that a person would bleed, sweat, and cry to achieve success. Melyssa is making the transition from video girl to real estate agent. During a meeting with her business manager, Melyssa admits how hard the transition is as they discuss her troubled finances. Despite her business manager's suggestion to return to the entertainment industry to make easy money, she stresses that she wants to make the real estate career work. The transition continues to be a difficult one. Her boss informs her that she needs to hustle harder, hang up the heels, and lose the attitude.

The successful careers of other women on *Blood, Sweat, and Heels* are also evident. Geneva explains that she and Demetria are media professionals. Although her mom wishes she had a more stable career, Geneva finds fulfillment in her chosen occupation. When Demetria meets with her mentor she explains that she is working on three book projects and a blog. She is shown planning an event to celebrate the 7-year anniversary of her blog and shooting a photo for the cover of her new book. Daisy hosts a dinner celebrating the digital re-launch of her book and also hosts a styling event.

In the remaining docusoaps that did not mention or allude to the women's industry/professional lives, professional Black women were still featured. Despite the docusoap's title, the women from *The Real Housewives of Atlanta* were far from your traditional, stay-at-home mothers. Cynthia is shown hosting a grand opening party for the new location of her (and her husband's) business. Kandi is shown casting, producing, and rehearsing for her first stage play (a project with her fiancé, Todd), *A Mother's Love*. Porsha is shown performing in the play. Kandi also discusses working on music for Grammy award winner Jennifer Hudson and working with her business partner in their clothing boutique.

Nene discusses the recent cancellation of her show *The New Normal* and is shown traveling for other business ventures. Tiffney from *Marrying the Game* is filmed interacting with her students and also working on a book project. Jackie from *Basketball Wives* is launching her own brand of cognac. The ladies of *SWV* and *Mary Mary* are shown rehearsing, traveling, in meetings with industry professionals, and performing. Rasheeda, Kalenna, and Karlie (*Love & Hip Hop Atlanta*) are also shown working on their music careers.

A Balancing Act

As professional women, many of the women have to engage in a balancing act. Some work to succeed in their career while also maintaining a relationship and/or raising their children. Although it isn't easy, some of the women do manage to maintain their careers while also tending to their children. This point is discussed in great detail in the chapter "Black Motherhood." Throughout the docusoaps you also see some examples of how the women must balance their careers with their relationships. In *Blood, Sweat, and Heels*, Demetria explains that she always wanted a career but now that her boyfriend is in the picture, she now wants a relationship and a career. But it is not always easy to balance her career and personal life, as she explains to her mentor while they have lunch. Daisy, from the same docusoap, is shown going on a date but makes it very clear to her date that her main priority at the time is her career and not a relationship.

Quad from *Married to Medicine* is another example of a woman who also faces questions about balancing careers and relationships. On their way to the couples' retreat to meet their friends, her husband, Greg, asks about Quad's ability to handle both her new company and their relationship.

> Greg: So babe how are you, how are you gonna, you know, tend to me and be this, you know, puppy couture mogul. I don't get it. How you gonna do that?
>
> Quad: Well you know that's when I have to put on my cape and be superwoman.

Without missing a step or showing any concern, Quad confidently declares that she will be able to act as if she has super powers and balance the two. Acknowledging that it will require super powers helps to illustrate that the balance is not easy. But her response also communicates her confidence in handling the problems. Greg also expresses his concerns with balancing work and relationship during the couples' retreat on *Married to Medicine*. Jackie's husband playfully raised her hand for her communicating that he feels she works too much.

Taj (*SWV: Reunited*) explains how a celebrity marriage is even tougher than a normal marriage, due in part to both of their hectic schedules. When her husband faces a potential job opportunity in New York, Taj is concerned as to how the move will impact her family and her career. She communicates this to her husband, stating how she feels she has always put her career on hold for the sake of his career. She feels it is now her turn. Although at the time her husband explains that he will take the job if offered, he ends up turning the job down so that Taj can focus on her career. Taj's comments as well as the couple's need for compromise helps demonstrate the difficulty in balancing careers and relationships.

Traci's husband feels that she has a problem juggling her career (and sisters) and her relationship. It is the subject of a couples' therapy activity where Traci is faced with a hypothetical ultimatum. She must choose between two doors—one that represents her career and sisters and one that represents her husband. The fact that the couple had to address this issue demonstrates the difficulty in balancing careers and relationships. However, the activity helped Traci realize that she had to spend more time with her husband even if she still pursues her career.

For some women, the balance is a bit different since they work with their husbands. Coko (*SWV: Reunited*), Erica (*Mary Mary*), and Kandi (*The Real Housewives of Atlanta*) are three examples of Black women who were shown working in their professional arena with their significant other. Other women show how they are able to balance their careers and relationships even if the topic is not discussed. It is quite possible that problems exist behind the scenes. For some of the women, their professional lives seem to threaten their relationships. As a standalone image, this could communicate that Black women are unable to balance both a career and personal life. However, the docusoaps presenting some of the women who were in relationships and maintaining careers communicate the idea that some of the women were able to handle the balance.

Ms. Independent

Quad and Mariah from *Married to Medicine* both stressed the importance of not being defined solely as a "doctor's wife." An underlying theme there is that the women desire their own independence. Quad discusses past relationships where the man attempted to control her with money, which serves as one of her motivations for maintaining her own independence and launching her own business. Viewers also learn about Quad's economic independence from her husband, Gregory, when they were at the couples' retreat and discussed their first date which involved shopping. Everyone was surprised to learn that Quad splurged on Gregory and not vice versa.

Simone experiences some financial troubles when she adopts a new accounting system for her medical practice. Her husband explains how he could have helped her if she had asked. However, she explains how it is difficult for her to run to her man when she needs help or is in trouble. Simone also makes it clear that she does not rely on a man for financial support. The quote that opens this section makes it clear that she makes her own money while also implying that cast member Toya does not have the same economic independence. Heavenly also makes comments during a dinner party that implies Toya is not financially independent and relies on her husband. The women boast about their independence, while criticizing Toya for what they perceive to be a lack of it. This communicates the importance of being independent, even when involved in a relationship. Their independence also continues to debunk some stereotypes. Although the Baby Momma character often has children for financial gain and the Gold Digger seeks men for their monetary value, many of these women had children and were in relationships while still maintaining their own financial security.

As Toya is the only wife on the show who does not have a career, this could also communicate a negative message about women who choose to be a housewife. Criticism of Toya, and the fact that the majority of the women across the docusoaps are not housewives, may deliver the message that being a housewife is not a respected job. Even though one of the docusoaps includes the word "housewives," none of the women on that show fulfills the requirements of being married and only working in the home.

Draya also makes it clear that she does not need a man for financial assistance. As a conversation between her and Ariane intensifies, Draya explains that she does not need to have kids by a man just to get a check. She is implying that Ariane is similar to a Baby Momma or Gold Digger and had children by a basketball player in order to secure financial stability. The comment was treated as an insult. Kandi's fiancé attempts to settle an issue between Kandi and her friend/assistant Carmon during an episode of *Kandi's Wedding*. Although he may have had good intentions, his actions lead to a conflict between the two friends. Kandi explains to Todd that she is a big girl and does not need his help solving her problems.

Kandi's financial independence is also made clear as she prepares for her wedding. She insists that her husband sign a prenuptial agreement in order to protect her many assets. When her fiancé objects to some of the terms in the agreement, they have a conflict and she even explains that the marriage will not take place if he does not sign the document. A similar point is made with Andrea and her fiancé in *Hollywood Exes*. Andrea chooses not to have her fiancée sign a prenuptial agreement and her friends are very concerned. They try to encourage her to use the legal agreement to protect her assets. Discussions of a prenuptial agreement inform the viewers that the women are financially independent from their fiancés.

Themes of independence were not only reserved for women within relationships. For Tiffney from *Marrying the Game*, her professional endeavors helped her redefine her independence after she ended her wedding engagement. She enjoys working on her book project partially because it is something she can do separately from her fiancé. Tanisha (*Marriage Boot Camp: Reality Stars*) showed her independence in her marriage even to the point where it negatively impacted her relationship. For example, on one episode Tanisha gets off of a phone call with her agent and is visibly excited. Her husband asks what happened and she brushes him off with a quick response. She then goes out into the hallway to share her news (in a bit more detail) with her houseguests. Her husband is bothered by her lack of communication. They also engaged in different discussions where they each discuss how her career (and their resulting attitudes) impacted their relationship. In the end, Tanisha admits that she chooses her career over her husband. They decide to divorce.

Community Outreach

Investing time and resources into projects outside of their jobs continues to demonstrate the women's professionalism and work ethic. Jackie and Lisa from *Married to Medicine* each launched organizations and events for the benefit of women. Jackie's annual "50 Shades of Pink" event educates women on health and breast cancer while also paying tribute to her patients who have battled the disease. Lisa spent time planning her Women's Empowerment Network conference—an event that helps women with personal and professional development.

Melyssa (*Blood, Sweat, and Heels*) tells Demetria about the book club that she started for young children. Melyssa invites Demetria to attend one of their meetings. Both women lead the children in a discussion on bullying, the influence of media, and sexual objectification. They attempt to encourage the children by providing them with a forum for open expression. Jackie (*Basketball Wives LA*) recruits the other cast members to help her event for the Lesbian, Gay, Bisexual, and Transgender (LGBT) community. The purpose of the program was to raise awareness for issues such as marriage equality.

Across all of the docusoaps, the majority of the women were shown working outside of the home whether it was in their chosen career or as community outreach. Although some of the women still choose to perform household tasks such as cooking and cleaning, they were not restricted to this role. In many cases the women were able to maintain their economic independence within their relationship because of their professions. Although it was not always easy, the women illustrated how they were able to balance their successful careers with relationships and/or children. The requirement for domesticity was not communicated; however, it is possible that women viewers received a negative message about those who choose to be housewives from watching these mediated depictions.

Always the Professional?

Many of the women were shown in their professional realm. Juggling careers, romantic relationships, and parenting was a constant routine for some. But there were some instances where the women's behavior related to their career or community outreach was unprofessional. For example, drama was no unusual occurrence in Kim's salon (*L.A. Hair*). In one episode, two of Kim's (White) employees have a physical altercation in the front of clients. On other occasions, the hair stylists (Black and White; male and female) are shown engaging in horseplay on the main floor of the salon. Although Kim is not engaging in these behaviors, the fact that it occurs in her workplace could be a reflection of her business practices.

L.A. Hair also featured the unprofessional behaviors of Malaka, the temporary receptionist. She is shown getting her nails done while at work, refusing to fulfill duties (taking out the trash), and arguing with a client. After accusing a male patron of being on drugs, the customer complained, and she was fired. She nonchalantly leaves the salon. Her lack of concern after being terminated, as well as her behavior at work, portrays an irresponsible and unprofessional employee.

During *Basketball Wives LA*, although the women joined together to work on Jackie's charity event, brainstorming meetings often turned into arguments over personal issues. In addition, some of the women felt that Jackie did not do a good job of delegating tasks and providing direction. So, although the women's participation in the event was commendable, there are some moments where they are seen behaving in an unprofessional manner.

On an episode of *Love & Hip Hop Atlanta*, Khadiyah engages in a heated exchange and eventual physical altercation, while serving as a real estate agent and showing a property. The tightly fitted dress Melyssa (*Blood, Sweat, and Heels*) wore while showing a rental property could also be considered unprofessional by some. Coko from *SWV Reunited* was bothered by Taj's behavior at one of their radio interviews. She considered Taj's constant laughter to be unprofessional and inappropriate for the situation.

So, in many instances the women were shown as successful businesswomen, yet there were some occasions when the women appeared to lack professionalism. What is promising is that this was not the only image that people see. Because there was a mix of positive and negative portrayals of the women's ability to work outside of the home, some could argue that the docusoaps provide a more realistic view of working lives of Black women.

· 8 ·

GIRL FIGHT

"Bitch, I'm gon give you a fuckin' collard green, cornbread, country ass whooping, ho."

— LO, *BAD GIRLS CLUB: CHICAGO*

Unfortunately, we cannot discuss images of Black women in reality television without considering the role of anger and conflict. This is one of the biggest critiques of reality television's representations for this group. Like sex, drama also sells. So, it was no surprise that there were examples of drama within the docusoaps. Dramatic situations are a normal part of an average person's life. However, the way in which Black women in docusoaps handle their drama will determine if stereotypical images such as Sapphire and the Angry Black Woman are perpetuated. The Angry Black Woman was present in the 2011 season. The characterization was also one of the reasons the public responded so negatively to Tami Roman, Evelyn Lozada, and *Basketball Wives*. Across the 2014 docusoaps there were still examples of drama ranging from minor disagreements to physical threats and attempted attacks.

The Intensity of Disagreements

Conflict within relationships is unavoidable; however, the conflict does not necessarily have to be destructive, confrontational, or damaging. The docusoaps featured examples of such conflicts that were quickly resolved and did not interrupt the relationships. For example, Porsha thanks Cynthia for coming to discuss an issue with her in private before the issues would have a chance to worsen. She explains how they handle the situation "grown woman style." Brie and Demetria (*Blood, Sweat, and Tears*) have a similar "grown woman style" conversation when Brie has an issue with one of the blogs Demetria wrote. They meet at a restaurant to calmly discuss the matter.

Simone and Quad (*Married to Medicine*), Erica and Tina (*Mary Mary*), and Kandi (*Kandi's Wedding*) had disagreements with their significant others about various topics. Although heated at the moment, ultimately the couples were able to overcome the disagreement and continue their relationship. Friends Ariane and Mimi (*Love & Hip Hop Atlanta*) engage in a heated argument about Mimi's sex tape release. Despite the disagreement, which involves yelling and tears at times, the women remain friends. Longtime friends Kandi and Carmon (*Kandi's Wedding*) had an intense argument over wedding plans that included tears and shouting. Although there was clearly tension, the women agreed to resolve the conflict and save their friendship by ending their working relationship. Even sisters Erica and Tina of *Mary Mary* had occasions where they engaged in conflict about their business decisions. But they, too, were able to overcome their issues.

But some disagreements were more intense. When telling her husband about a conflict between Nene and Marlo (*Real Housewives of Atlanta*), Phaedra explained that the situation got "hoodlicious." The women were yelling and throwing insults at each other during Cynthia's event, The Bailey Bowl. The situation was dissolved as Nene began to walk away and others helped to put space between the two women. However, their public disagreement puts a damper on Cynthia's event. Nene was also involved in a heated conversation with another cast member—Kenya. At another one of Cynthia's events (the opening of her new business space), the women engage in a public argument. Eventually, Peter (Cynthia's husband) comes to pull Nene away from the conflict. Although Kenya attempts to follow Nene and continue the conversation, the situation is dissolved. Yet it does not end without first interrupting a formal event. Quad and Mariah (*Married to Medicine*) also engaged in conflict while in public and at a friend's event. In one episode, the two women are standing outside of the venue arguing about their failed relationship and who was at fault. It takes outside parties to separate the women in order to end the conflict.

The tension between Carmon and Tan was pretty evident on the docusoap *Kandi's Wedding*. So, for some it may have come as no surprise that the two engaged in a verbal altercation. While in the middle of a restaurant with the bridal party (they were there planning Kandi's bachelorette party), the two disagree about Carmon's relationship (or lack thereof) with Momma Joyce. While Tan tries to reprimand Carmon for her past interactions with Momma Joyce, Carmon responds in a hostile way that intensifies the conflict.

Carmon: Bye, Felicia.
Phaedra: Well who is Felicia?
Carmon: The random bitch you don't give a fuck about.

Carmon's reference to Tan as "Felicia" is borrowed from the popular film, *Friday* featuring Ice Cube and Chris Tucker. In the film, Ice Cube's character dismisses a female drug addict who continues to visit his porch asking for handouts.

Tan returns the insult by calling Carmon a bitch. The women begin to yell at each other in the middle of the restaurant. It takes other members of the bridal party to calm the situation down. Kandi's cousin Weenie even uses her own anger to address their inappropriate behavior: "…if somebody mess up my cousin's wedding, I promise you they gon have to deal with me!" Interestingly, Weenie inserts a threat into an ongoing conflict in order to put an end to the argument and protect her cousin's special day. These open altercations may communicate that Black women "don't know how to act" when in public, due in part to their aggressiveness and anger.

The hostility between Brittish and Brandi also seemed to build pretty early. Brittish interpreted some of Brandi's comments about her husband as being offensive. The two engage in an argument while at a restaurant with the other ladies. However, their conflict intensifies during Brittish's Turkish Tea Party, which she hosted at her house. As the ladies begin to rehash the events from their first rocky encounter, tempers flare. Brittish tells Brandi, "The first day I met you I knew you one of them bitches I don't like." Brandi calls Brittish insecure, while Brittish feels Brandi has a superiority complex. As Brandi and Sundy decide to separate from the group to discuss their own issues that transpired at a different event, the conflict between Brandi and Brittish only gets worse. The two stand up and begin to face each other as some of the other women quickly move to get in between them. Brittish yells, "I'm not gonna put my hands on you" however by that time she has already kicked off her shoes.

There is no proof that Brittish removed her shoes in order to fight, but that specific action in the midst of an argument can indicate a person is preparing for physical altercation. It is similar to the stereotypical "removing of the earrings." Viewers learn that Brandi had hoped to engage in physical combat with Brittish. As she discussed the events with Malaysia and Draya, she explains how she wanted to "beat the living daylights out of Brittish."

Like Brittish, Geneva (*Married to Medicine*) also displays conflicting actions and words when involved in conflict. The women gather together for dinner at Mica's house. They all recognize the tension in the air as some of them are upset by Demetria's blog post. At the dinner, Geneva explains that she does not fight because she is a grown woman. However, as the women start to discuss the issue of the blog and Geneva expresses her concerns, she tells Demetria that if it happens again, "it will be a problem." Of course, she does not explicitly threaten to fight Demetria so what she means by "problem" is left open for interpretation. Yet, the context may lead some people to think that she threatened some type of violent behavior. Later, Geneva is involved in another conflict with Mica. She explains that she is leaving the event before she hits Mica. She then goes on to explain that a lady knows when to leave. While her threat to Demetria is more vague, her physical threat towards Mica is clear.

Hollywood Exes also featured a heated exchange during a group dinner. Following a dispute between two of the women, Andrea decides to call everyone together for dinner in an attempt to mediate the situation. As the dinner commences, several arguments begin. Cast member Mayte engages in disagreements with three of the Black women—Nicole, Sheree, and the original mediator, Andrea. While hashing out their issues Mayte comments that her experiences with parenting as a single mother are more difficult than those of Sheree, who has the financial support of her celebrity ex-husband. Andrea becomes enraged and begins to yell at Mayte about how such a statement is unfair and hurtful in an exchange between friends.

Although Andrea storms out, the argument between Nicole and Mayte reconvenes as they take turns yelling and calling each other a bitch. What began as a peaceful dinner quickly turned into an argument in the restaurant. When discussing the incident on a different occasion, Nicole explains how she is embarrassed about her actions and what took place. One of her friends and cast members, Jessica, says to her: "I've never seen you flare up like that," indicating that this was not normal behavior for Nicole. Shanna, another cast member, commented on Andrea's behavior: "I think I saw Drea's true colors more than anything because I could see that she can be very friendly and very cool but you know if you say the wrong thing, she can switch on a dime."

Those Are Fighting Words

Some of the conflicts were so intense that they almost amounted to a fight. There was no physical altercation because others prevented a fight and not because of the women's own self-control. *The Real Housewives of Atlanta* featured an incident that had blogs, social media, and radio stations buzzing after the episode aired. Nene decided to host a lingerie-themed party for the women and their significant others. (Porsha was still present and attended the party with her sister.) After a physical fight ensued between two of the male guests, the tension in the room quickly thickened.

While trying to make sense of the first altercation, Kandi decided to confront a few of the attendees about their comments that implied that her fiancé was an opportunist. This turned into an intense exchange between Kandi and Cynthia and eventually a violent outburst from Kandi. She later explains that the reason for her reaction was the fact that Mallory (Cynthia's sister) had touched her inappropriately. Kandi is quickly separated from Cynthia, Peter, and Mallory. She screams across the room, "I will drag that ho!" Other attendees are able to calm the situation down enough to the point where all parties are separated and there is no actual fight. Because of her actions, Cynthia and Peter describe Kandi as "ghetto" and "a street thug." Kandi even acknowledges that her behavior was inappropriate and she is embarrassed. She decides to apologize to the other women by inviting them to a spa day and discussing the problem. In a confessional, she explains that she is not normally a violent person: "I'm a don't start none won't be done type of person. But once you start it, I'm going to finish it." While her actions were violent and outrageous, the shame she attached to those behaviors helps communicate the idea that such actions are not appropriate.

Kandi's mother is involved in a similar situation with Todd's mother, Sharon, in an episode of *Kandi's Wedding*. With the wedding quickly approaching, Kandi and Todd decide to host a dinner for both of their mothers. Tension is expected, as Sharon is unhappy with the way Momma Joyce treats her son.

In addition, Momma Joyce has made it very clear that she is not a big fan of Todd or his mother. As they sit at dinner, Momma Joyce explains how she is not allowed to spend the night at her daughter's house although Todd's mom is in town and staying there for several days. Todd and Kandi chime in to explain why this is not the case and the situation quickly turns into an argument between Sharon and Momma Joyce.

As Sharon tries to lunge across the table to where Joyce is seated, she angrily says, "You got the wrong one now bitch." Todd and Kandi have to physically hold their mothers back while each professes their desire to fight. Momma Joyce says, "I wanna whoop her ass" while Sharon tells her son "I was getting ready to punch her in her face." After things have calmed down, all parties reconvene and Sharon apologizes for calling Momma Joyce a bitch. She then explains that she reacted in order to protect her son. The next day when discussing the fight with Kandi and her hair stylist, Momma Joyce issues one more threat about Sharon: "Well, she gonna be in a coma if she ever try that again."

Basketball Wives LA also features some "close to fighting" action while the ladies are in Paris. Sundy attempts to mediate some ongoing tensions between Jackie and Malaysia. She is happy to see that Malaysia accepts her invitation to join her, Jackie, and Brittish for breakfast. However, when Malaysia and Brandi arrive, suffering from a hangover, and Malaysia is unwilling to discuss her issues with Jackie, Sundy becomes upset. Malaysia and Brandi decide to leave the gathering, which triggers an argument with Sundy. The opening quote for this section is an example of one of the statements Malaysia makes to Sundy. She references a past physical altercation between Sundy and Draya and also explains her willingness to also "put hands on" (to hit) her. The women eventually separate.

When Brandi learns that Sundy attacked her because of her infertility issues, Brandi becomes enraged and charges downstairs. Malaysia tries to pull Brandi back and calm her down. She reminds Brandi that they have "too much to lose" and should not engage in an altercation with Sundy. Brandi, who is very emotional—crying and yelling—tries to break loose of Malaysia's hold while throwing insults at Sundy. She tells Brittish to deliver the message to Sundy that she plans to fight her every time she sees her.

Violence was not limited to interactions between females or between enemies, for that matter. Tanisha from *Marriage Boot Camp: Reality Stars* and Gloria from *Marriage Boot Camp* are the aggressors in physical altercations with their spouses. The men are not shown hitting their wives; however, both

Tanisha and Gloria are shown hitting their husbands during an argument. Tanisha even taunts her husband by repeatedly telling him to hit her. Viewers of both shows may not be surprised by the women's behaviors. Each woman was also explained by other cast members as being loud and/or aggressive towards her spouse.

Bad Girls Club: Chicago and *Love & Hip Hop Atlanta* featured Black women actually engaging in physical altercations. For example, the opening quote of this chapter is from an episode where Lo fights with a White cast member. Not only does Lo threaten to hurt her during an argument, she eventually runs up to her and hits her before being pulled away. She shows no shame for her actions. In fact, the feud with the cast member continues throughout the season. Even in instances when the "bad girls" were not directly in the fight, they still sometimes expressed their approval of the violent actions. For example, in one episode two (White/non-Black) cast members engage in a fight. When discussing the fight, Blu said "Lindsey jumps at Jada and got in her bubble so Jada did what she had to do. Bap, bap." Her comments imply that Jada's actions in the fight were understandable since her space was violated.

On *Love & Hip Hop Atlanta*, Karlie engages in a fight with Black cast member Khadiyah. From the same show, Bambi punches Black cast member Erica P. at a nightclub. In both scenarios, the women are fighting over a guy. Of course, this is even more troubling. Although conflict and anger were certainly present throughout the docusoaps, luckily actual physical fighting was not a common theme across the shows. Yet, even this small amount is problematic for Black women who are constantly dealing with the image of the Angry Black Woman. Furthermore the aggressive behaviors and threats of physical violence can also reinforce the belief that Black women are angry.

Can Women Get Along?

The catfight is common in television programming and, as Pozner (2010) argued, reality television appears to be no exception to the rule. The disputes mentioned above could continue to reflect this girl vs. girl mentality. After all, the majority of the disputes were among the female members of the main cast. However, it is important to note that the women were not only featured engaging in catfights. Even if there were cases where all of the Black female cast members could not get along together, there were still friendships within the larger group. And, as discussed earlier, some of the disagreements featured in the docusoaps occurred among friends. This healthy and expected type of conflict did not interrupt the women's friendships. In addition, there were several examples of friendships where the women interacted, provided support, showed concern, and had fun. On *Marrying the Game* Tiffney is shown interacting with multiple Black female friends who allowed her to vent about her children and failed engagement. In fact, it was her friend and coworker who first advised her to journal about her experiences to help with her healing. This journaling helped her come up with the idea for her book project.

The castmates of *Hollywood Exes* had a strong friendship. In fact, Nicole, Shamecka, and Sheree served as bridesmaids for Andrea's wedding. The women were shown laughing and having fun on multiple occasions, including the girls' trip to Hawaii. Brittish, Jackie, and Sundy had fun together as they explored Paris. When Jackie first saw the finished product of her cognac venture, Sundy became emotional because she was so happy that her friend's dream has come to life. On *Married to Medicine*, Lisa feels comfortable confiding in Jackie about her medical condition. The ladies of *SWV* are shown laughing and joking with each other while on the road. These are only a few examples of the ways the women supported each other and enjoyed the friendship. Like the women in the 2011 seasons, the Black women featured in the 2014 docusoaps are capable of interacting with other Black women in ways that do not have to result in conflict—even in the midst of a drama-filled storyline.

· 9 ·

WHO IS SHE REPPING?

Earlier we discussed La La Anthony's written piece on her racial identity. La La decided to release her essay in response to several questions about her racial identity; she was often asked if she were Black. She confirmed that she was Latina. But the fact that La La was often questioned about her ethnicity is an example of how racial ambiguity and social construction of race are factors when studying and discussing women of color.

After researching reality television dating shows, Dubrofsky (2011) concluded that reality television shows often cast racially ambiguous members, whose ethnicity or racial background is not easily discernible. More specifically, racial ambiguity refers to participants who are not labeled as a specific race on the show. In these situations, the individuals' appearance can be construed as one or more races even if he or she is not actually a member of the race(s) that viewers attribute to them. If a woman in a reality television show "is not marked physically as a woman of color, the series can represent her ethnicity in a mutable fashion" (Dubrofsky, 2011, p. 31). Regardless of the race these ambiguous characters claim or identify with, producers are able to use these women to "signify several women of color" (p. 32). Viewers then see the ambiguous women as a representation of their specific racial and ethnic groups (Dubrofsky, 2011; Ono, 2008; Valdivia, 2005).

La La's essay illuminates the complexities of the social construction of race and highlights how viewers may decide an "ambiguous" woman's racial identity on their own. She has publicly identified herself as Latina; however, some still may view her as a Black woman. As illustrated earlier, the term Hispanic or Latina ignores "the diversity and complexity of the racial categories of the 20 nationalities" Hispanic or Latina represents (Vargas, 2008, p. 952). So while, La La chooses to avoid racial politics by choosing to be viewed as Latina, that rhetorical positioning does not change the fact that in a racialized society, she is still "raced"; as such, viewers are likely to still view her as Black. In previous chapters, we examined women who at least *appeared* Black and did not self-identify as otherwise. Yet, in this chapter we also consider the portrayals of other women of color who were identified as or self-identified as a race other than Black but who may be socially considered representations of Black women. Because of La La's experiences, it is important that we also consider other participants of Spanish descent.

Spanish Culture

La La Anthony (*La La's Full Court Life*), Aysia Garza (*Bad Girls Club: Chicago*), and Joseline Hernandez (*Love & Hip Hop Atlanta*) all have ethnic ties to Spanish culture. La La identifies herself as Latina. Aysia's last name—Garza—is a surname of Spanish descent (in fact in Spanish language it means heron). Joseline Hernandez constantly self-identifies as "the Puerto Rican princess." Although these women are Latinas, we argue that viewers may see them as representations of Black women based on their phenotypical characteristics.

Throughout the docusoaps, viewers learn different details about the women's lives and personalities. In *La La's Full Court Life*, La La is shown working on her new clothing line. In one episode La La attends a meeting and finds that she is ill prepared to undertake such a challenging task. She admits that the endeavor is difficult, but she works harder and tries to learn from her mistakes. La La sends the message that a woman of color can be successful both inside and outside of her home. Despite her career, she is often shown interacting with her son Kiyan. She is not the stereotypical baby momma who carelessly has children for financial gain and does not have a relationship with the father. In fact, La La is married to the father of her child and is often shown interacting with their son. Her financial success can probably be assumed before viewing the show. After all, she is a successful television personality, actress, and married to a famous NBA player. In addition, her reality television show has been in the works for several seasons. However, viewers also see examples of her financial success throughout the show. For example, in one episode La La rents a cabin so that she and her friends (and her son) could spend time together.

La La also shows how women can have healthy relationships. She interacts with several women, especially her cousin Dice and her close friend Po. This is not to say that the women do not have conflicts. In one episode, Dice and La La have a disagreement over Dice's new girlfriend. However, the two eventually reconcile. As for her appearance, she has a lighter skin tone, long hair, light eyes, and a voluptuous shape, which is highlighted by the form-fitting clothing she often wears.

Joseline from *Love & Hip Hop Atlanta* is arguably one of the better-known and controversial characters of the docusoap. She is shown feuding with several of her cast members, including the mother of her husband's child, Mimi. Joseline is not shy about her sexuality. In fact, she is heard bragging about her sex appeal. While preparing for a photo spread in a magazine, she tells Tammy that it is important that she shows ass. According to Mimi, Joseline is quite promiscuous. When discussing Joseline's criticism of the sex tape, Mimi tells Nikko: "Joseline got more miles on her (expletive) than 8 of me. ..." Although the word is bleeped out for viewers, it is clear Mimi is discussing Joseline's sexual organs.

Joseline is also quite the firecracker. In addition to her verbal and physical altercations with other women, she has a heated exchange with her husband. When discussing his infidelity and the possibility of her catching a sexually transmitted disease she threatens: "You're gon be six feet (expletive) under and I'm gonna be in *The First 48*. ..." Of course, Joseline could be being sarcastic as she threatens to kill her husband; *The First 48* is a popular reality show that follows homicide units in different cities. Some would even consider her anger and use of sarcasm to be appropriate since she had recently heard about her husband's alleged infidelities. But because of Joseline's past verbal and physical altercations with other cast members, the heated exchange with her husband may be viewed as yet another example of her aggressive behaviors.

Throughout the docusoap, Joseline is also shown working on her career in the music industry and is shown interacting with women. For example, she visits her friend K. Michelle in New York and is shown with Tammy while shopping and preparing for an upcoming photo shoot. However, other cast members later discuss Joseline's character as a friend with Tammy, who is new to the show and is only hanging out with Joseline for the first time. Mimi warns Tammy that Joseline will "stab her in the back." Tammy also admits that Joseline "throws jabs" or rather, insults, while they are interacting.

Aysia only appeared for one season on *Bad Girls Club: Chicago*. She was a housemate who was unable to finish the rest of that season. Aysia received mixed reviews. Many of the castmates had issues with her presence and actions. Throughout the season she was involved in verbal and/or physical altercations with castmates but managed to create a bond with some of the women, especially Blu.

When Aysia arrives in the house, she is involved in a romantic relationship with her boyfriend in her hometown. Blu is also involved in a relationship (although sometimes she does not label it as such) with a woman at home named Diamond. However, Asyia and Blu engage in a flirtatious relationship while living in the Bad Girls Club house. The two are often shown sleeping in the same bed, cuddling, and Aysia later reveals that the two have kissed. When on the phone with her boyfriend, Aysia jokingly refers to Blu as her girlfriend. Although both Blu and Aysia are involved in relationships with other people, it is Aysia who is most often criticized. When Aysia begins sharing details about her relationship with Blu with people outside the house (including a friend of Diamond's friend), Redd says that Aysia needs to "know her place" and "control her feelings." This alludes to the fact that it is okay for Aysia to be the extra woman in the relationship if she understands her "role" as the "side" woman.

Other Racially Ambiguous Characters

Lisa Nicole Cloud first appears on *Married to Medicine* during the docusoap's second season. Her husband is a doctor but she is not financially dependent on him because she is a successful entrepreneur. Throughout the docusoap she is shown working on her own career while inspiring other women to do the same. She offers advice to Quad on her new business venture. Lisa also spent time planning her Women's Empowerment Network Conference—an event that helps women with personal and professional development. She is also shown (as earlier discussed) having healthy relationships with other women, which includes open girl talk about her sexuality (with her husband).

Like La La, Lisa is shown interacting with her children in addition to her professional life. Her care and concern for her children are illustrated, especially during her health scare. When Lisa learns that the mass in her breast may be cancer, her major concern is her children. In a confessional she explains:

> I know I'm strong and I know that if this is cancer, I can handle that. But what worries me is my kids because if I ever had to be here without my mother I don't know what I would do and the thought that my kids could have to grow up without their mom. That's just a lot to think about right now.

Even when facing a health scare, Lisa selflessly focuses her attention on the impact the situation may have on her children. She is also not your stereotypical Baby Momma, since she is still married to the father of her children despite his previous infidelities.

Mica Hughes from *Blood, Sweat, and Heels* is the quintessential embodiment of the racially ambiguous character. In fact, upon first review of the cast member page, we instantly classified her as Non-black and did not include her in the original analysis. During our first review of the docusoap episodes, we watched as Mica's mother, who did appear to be Black, visited. Mica is, in fact, a Black woman, and she was included in our general discussion on Black women in docusoaps. However, we must also feature her here in this discussion because of her ambiguous appearance.

Mica is involved in ongoing friendships and feuds with the other female cast members. There seems to be a divide in the group, and a lot of the issues deal with Mica's behavior at a previous gathering. After recently losing her father, Mica attends one of Brie's events, at which some of the women feel that Mica acted erratically. Throughout the season, many of the conversations focus on Mica's behavior at that event as well as at other events. Brie and Geneva feel that Mica has a drinking problem. Mica is intoxicated and flashing her legs open at a public event. Geneva says she is "loud and obnoxious" and feels she is aggressive and potentially violent.

Mica has her share of conflicts with Brie, Geneva (especially), and Demetria, but she is also shown having happier interactions with Melyssa and Brie. For example, after a stressful day at work Melyssa chooses to visit and confide in Mica. When Brie has an important event, Mica comes to support her friend. Mica also hosts a dinner party for all of the girls and is also shown in a relationship with her live-in boyfriend. When her mother visits and they discuss Mica's romantic relationship, her mother mentions how Mica wants to become a "Baby Momma." But, Mica is quick to correct her mother and explain that she wants to be a *wife*.

Implications of the Social Construction of Race

Audience members could view each of these women—La La, Joseline, Asyia, Lisa, and Mica—in different ways. To some, they may be clear representations of Black women. However, others may consider them the opposite. When considering race as a social construction, individuals will consider several different factors before deciding if a woman is Black. Viewers may consider the women's appearances, interactions, and comparisons to self. For example, if I am a Black female viewer and Lisa looks like me—or Mica does not look like me—that may impact whether I view either as a representation of all Black women.

If the women are considered representations of Black women, they align with many of the themes that we found throughout our analysis. Lisa and La La are both shown as professional women of color who tend to their children and maintain a successful relationship with their husbands. All of the women are also shown as being friends with other women. Although Mica, Aysia, and Joseline have a large amount of conflict within their shows, there are some instances where the women are involved in healthy interactions with other women. Thus, the women do share similarities with the other Black women examined here. In this regard, their presentations would reinforce the positive messages communicated by the other portrayals.

Yet, this could also have an adverse effect. Even if the women are not Black but viewed as belonging to the racial group by some audience members, their negative portrayals could serve as unflattering representations for this group. Although we know that race is not a monolithic group or categorization, portions of the viewing population do not make such sophisticated distinctions when they watch television. Thus, when we consider Joseline and her portrayal on *Love & Hip Hop Atlanta*, her volatile behavior could be considered a representation of Black women despite her self-identification as the "Puerto Rican princess." Hence, the notion that "all" Black women are Angry Black Women.

· 1 0 ·
WHY ARE VIEWERS CALLING FOR BOYCOTTS?

Qualitative researchers often look for dominant themes that emerge from the analysis of data (Lucas & D'Enbeau, 2013). Using a qualitative perspective, we discussed dominant themes in the presentation of Black women in docusoaps and the various ways that viewers could interpret those presentations. Qualitative research often provides rich, thick description of the phenomenon under investigation. So when dominant themes emerge, they are revealing because of the repetition they present. In the preceding chapters, we have established that in totality, the images of Black women in reality television docusoaps are more positive than negative. Conflict was present in many instances, which has the potential to reinforce the Angry Black Woman stereotype. As mentioned earlier, this is troubling as it is an image that continues to find its way in media representations of Black women. But, many of the images found within the docusoaps were presented in a flattering light (e.g., professional women, working mothers). There are also some images that may result in multiple readings, depending on the audience. For example, the women's sexuality could be viewed as natural expression or hypersexuality. Yet, the balance of these images and the possibility for different interpretations is steps away from a stereotypical cast of one-dimensional Black female characters.

In this chapter, however, we turn the tables a bit. We have already highlighted the dominant themes. We must now acknowledge some aspects of these docusoaps that were not dominant themes but are noteworthy because they were hot topics for discussion by viewers. This is important for various reasons:

1. Although a specific characteristic mentioned below may not have been dominant or omnipresent across the shows we analyzed, each of the Black women featured on a docusoap could be (and likely is) considered a representation of Black women. Thus, viewers could use all behaviors witnessed, even if these behaviors only occurred in a few shows or a few instances, to construct their reality and their perceptions of Black women as a whole.
2. Research in marketing, public relations, and management communication shows that a consumer is likely to be more vocal about a negative experience than a positive experience. Thus, this might provide a context and rationale for much of the negative attention that these docusoaps receive—especially in the form of viewers calling for boycotts of this programming.

In this chapter, we highlight some of the "outliers" in our analysis. When we use the term outlier, we are referring to the women or characteristics of those women that did not have a high occurrence among the majority of the shows but are still connected to the stereotypical characterizations of Black women. We also note that it is possible (but not likely) these images and characteristics were stressed more in episodes that were not the ones randomly selected for our analysis.

He's My Man!

Throughout the docusoaps, the women were shown when they were dealing with conflict. These conflicts included but were not limited to: disagreements about business decisions and issues with their children. Some of these conflicts were resolved more productively than others. A few of the women had disputes about "possession" of men. We mentioned some of these conflicts briefly in the discussion of drama in the docusoaps. However, we want to highlight the conflicts over the "possession" of men here, specifically, because these conflicts can accentuate the common stereotypes about Black women's promiscuity. For example, *Love & Hip Hop Atlanta* features women physically fighting over men, and the "outside" woman uses her feminine wiles to lure the (un)suspecting man away from the woman he is partnered with (or belongs to). We also recognize that the man likely plays an equal or greater role in an extramarital/relationship; yet, what is highlighted in these shows are the women's "battles" over the men. We highlight here Khadiyah and Karlie because they were shown arguing and physically fighting over a man. In the same docusoap, viewers see Bambi and Erica P. fight over issues that stem from a man's multiple relationships.

In both of these instances, one of the women is framed as the "mistress." For example, Bambi is often filmed with her significant other, Scrappy. While Scrappy's mother is aware of his relationship with Bambi, she and Bambi are unaware of his relationship with Erica P. Scrappy refers to Erica P. as a "friend" and acknowledges that Bambi did not know about their friendship. Erica P. reveals that Scrappy sends her flirtatious text messages that are not normal for two individuals who are just friends. This is similarly the case for Khadiyah and Karlie, as Khadiyah is originally portrayed as "the other woman." Despite the men's infidelities and disloyal behaviors, the women still fight with each other.

On *The Real Housewives of Atlanta* there is a lot of friction between Kenya and Phaedra. Phaedra complains of inappropriate interactions between her husband, Apollo, and Kenya. These issues are one of the reasons why Phaedra refers to Kenya on the show as "Keyna Moore Whore." It certainly is troubling that women were fighting over a man. This negative portrayal of Black women not only communicates something about relationships, it also carries meaning about the women's sexuality. In each scenario, the woman presented as "the other woman" may also be viewed as a hypersexual character because of her willingness to pursue a man who is already involved in a relationship. This especially reinforces the girl-vs-girl mentality that Pozner (2010) argued is exhibited by the reality television catfight. The positive conclusion that we draw from this study is that this theme (He's my man/stealing my man) was not dominant across all of the docusoaps. However, we wonder if the image is one of the most memorable. We must acknowledge that this image does exist and has the potential to impact viewers' construction of reality.

The Hypersexual Black Woman

Lelee's (*SWV Reunited*) casual attitude toward sex has been discussed in preceding chapters. Again, she was not criticized for her behaviors and she was not ashamed of her sex life. When discussing an upcoming date, she even expresses how she wants to approach sex and relationships differently. Yet, it is possible that viewers consider Lelee's behavior to be inappropriate and promiscuous. During their therapy sessions, Traci and Tanisha (*Marriage Boot Camp: Reality Stars*) both admitted infidelities. However, the act itself was not discussed. Discussions centered more on repairing the relationship despite the infidelity. Both women accused their husbands of infidelity as well. But again, viewers could read the women's unfaithfulness as promiscuous behavior.

Kalenna's (*Love & Hip Hop Atlanta*) open relationship with both her husband and her best friend Ashley, may also yield mixed interpretations. On one hand, despite her sexual relationship with her best friend, Kalenna was not being unfaithful to her husband because he was aware of the women's relationship and sometimes joined in. Yet the desire for such a nontraditional relationship could be perceived by some as hypersexual.

Bad Girls Club, in 2011, was a primary source of the promiscuous Black woman motif. Sadly, in 2014 the show still produced images that could be perceived in the same way. One could argue that, based on the title of the show, what else should one expect? But we wonder if viewers perceive that all of the women on this show are promiscuous, or do they see that only the Black women on this show are promiscuous? That distinction is not a minor one, especially if these shows are one of the few ways in which some non-Black viewers experience/encounter Black women and/or Black life. So to clarify that point, we will highlight how some of the Black women are depicted on the show.

To begin the 2014 season, Redd admits to sleeping with her sister's husband. She explains how she does not feel guilty and blames her behavior on the rude treatment she received from her sister (e.g., insults). She also acknowledges that her sister did not know what was going on before she explained this to her new roommate on the show. Despite her behavior, Redd quickly tries to explain that she is not promiscuous: "It's not like, ok I go around sleeping with everybody's husband. That's just nasty. I didn't even enjoy it." But her statement (that she didn't enjoy it) conflicts with her confession.

Blu, also from *Bad Girls Club: Chicago*, exhibits behaviors that can be construed as hypersexual and promiscuous. Although her roommates do not focus on criticizing her behaviors, a life coach attempts to help Blu with her commitment issues. Throughout the series, Blu maintains some type of relationship with two women. She enters the house involved (at some level, as she often proclaims she is single) with Diamond. While living in the Bad Girls' house she begins a flirtatious relationship with her roommate, Aysia. In one episode Blu says that she does plan to tell Diamond the true details about the relationship with Aysia; however, she plans to wait until after the experience on the show—clearly to benefit her self-interests. Her manipulative behavior highlights her promiscuous behavior. Although her work with the life coach could be seen as positive, it is counteracted by the fact that she continues both relationships throughout the season.

One shared thread between Kalenna, Blu, and Redd is that each woman is bisexual. All three ladies are shown pursuing other women. However, they also state that they are or are shown to be in relationships with men. This combined with their behavior has the potential to communicate a demeaning message about their sexuality. Some viewers may use these portrayals to reinforce the stereotype that bisexual people are promiscuous. Thus, Black gayness or bisexuality is deemed abnormal, has no place in a "normal" society, and warrants professional counseling and treatment. Although hypersexuality was not a dominant theme, these few instances do have the potential to impact viewers' perceptions and could trigger viewers to call for more responsible representations of Black women on these shows.

Momma Dee

Love & Hip Hop Atlanta introduced many to rap artist Scrappy's mother who is known as Momma Dee. Her actions have earned her a section to herself. It is hard to characterize Momma Dee's behavior in just one category. Her son, Scrappy, proclaims that he is the Prince of the South. This is a title that Momma Dee has taken quite literally. In many episodes she refers to herself as the queen, her home and life as the palace, and she often calls the "guards" to handle individuals who displease her. Momma Dee's actions communicate her false sense of royalty and superiority.

Momma Dee's love for Scrappy is evident. She is critical of the other people in his life. In fact, she refers to his girlfriend as "the Bambi" and is rude to her until Bambi reveals she is pregnant (but Bambi later suffers a miscarriage). The way in which she refers to Bambi can certainly be considered a form of disrespect. Even when her son is in blatantly wrong, Momma Dee stands by his side. For example, when Scrappy's philandering actions catch up with him, leading to a physical altercation between Bambi and Erica P., Momma Dee makes no reference to his wrongdoing. Instead, she explains to her son that he needs to "control [his] bitches." Momma Dee's statement is problematic in many ways. First, she implies that a man should control a woman. Second, she puts the blame on the women and not on her son, who is the cause of the fight.

In one episode, Scrappy asks his mother if she has taken the medication that helps control her bipolar disorder. However, we cannot assume that her behavior can be attributed to her mental disorder. In fact, Momma Dee continues to refer to herself as royalty and brings up the "guards" and "palace" after confirming that she did take her medication for the day. With *Love & Hip Hop Atlanta* being such a highly rated show, many view (and probably discuss) Momma Dee's behavior. Her false sense of entitlement, treatment/discussion of other women, and aggressive role in her son's life have the potential to communicate a negative message. Although she is one of a kind, her presence could influence audience views on how they look at and treat Black women in society.

We argue that such negative outliers probably overshadow other neutral and/or positive outliers. We highlight two of those outliers here.

Influences of Faith

Faith was not a large part of the storylines across majority of the docusoaps. However, there were instances within the different shows where Black women spoke about their faith. In *SWV Reunited*, Coko is shown pursuing her gospel career. When her family faces a tough time and attends court with her son, her pastor also attends. The singing group Mary Mary is filmed continuing their careers as gospel artists. In addition, Tina discusses how gospel music helps her heal from her husband's infidelity. Heavenly from *Married to Medicine* makes her religious belief clear. On more than one occasion she discusses how she and her castmates should "praise Jesus." She also explains that her dedication and submission to her husband are inspired by her religious beliefs. Toya, from the same docusoap, also discusses how she prays in order to help deal with the stress brought on by their search for a new house.

As Brandi discusses her battle with ovarian cancer, she acknowledges her faith and how it gave her strength. Daisy (*Blood, Sweat, and Heels*) prays for a successful event while Tiffney (*Marrying the Game*) is shown praying with her children before bedtime. Kandi (*Kandi's Wedding*) and her fiancé Todd are shown attending marriage counseling with a pastor before their nuptials. In each of these instances, the women are presented as spiritual beings. Although their faith did not dominate the storylines, these behaviors can communicate to the audience that the women do have some belief in a higher power, which provides them (both the women in the series and the viewers) with inspiration.

The Dutiful Housewife

Many of the shows featured Black women working and earning their own money as a indication of their independence. Even *The Real Housewives of Atlanta* did not feature a traditional Black housewife. Yet there is a housewife featured in *Married to Medicine*—Toya is married to a doctor. Instead of working outside of the home, she takes care of the domestic duties including cooking, cleaning, and taking care of their two young children. Although some of her castmates have made comments about her financial dependence on her husband (as discussed earlier), Toya stresses that she is proud of her job as a wife and mother. She is also shown collaborating with her husband on family business. For example, the two discuss plans and attend meetings for their upcoming move to their new house. So although she is a housewife, she plays a key role in major family (business) decisions.

Her fellow cast member, Heavenly, works outside of the home as a dentist. However, she prides herself on also taking care of her family (husband and their children) and their home. In fact, Heavenly was very adamant that all women should fulfill the domestic chores in their home. In her opinion, tending to the home, caring for the children, and submitting to her husband are part of a woman's responsibilities. This position might resonate with some viewers who ascribe to traditional, religious family values. Heavenly (we wonder if there is irony here in her name) felt this was especially important for women who did not work outside of the home. For example, when Toya's husband cooks breakfast during a couples' retreat, Heavenly criticizes Toya. She explains that cooking for her husband is the least Toya should do since she does not work outside of the home. Heavenly also hosts a dinner party where the theme is "relationships." During the dinner she tries to encourage all of the women to be more submissive and domestic. However, since she does work outside of the home it appears that Heavenly believes in a more nontraditional view of the housewife. Her interaction with other cast members and the audience reveals that she feels women should find success inside and outside of the home.

The dutiful housewife theme was not dominant throughout the shows. Those who criticize the overly negative images of Black women in docusoaps might see this image as positive. Others might see it as antiquated. Others might view it as negative, but not as negative as the hypersexual woman. More specifically, audience members may read the criticism of Toya's status, as well as the lack of housewives in other shows, as meaning that the role of the housewife is negative. In terms of Heavenly's comments, some viewers may agree with her statements wholeheartedly, while others may view her comments in relation to the many images of Black women who were not necessarily submissive to their husbands. Regardless of how these images are interpreted, we do not believe that this outlier outshines the previous outliers mentioned.

CONCLUSION

Reality television makes a false promise to present reality to its audiences. However this medium has the power to educate its audiences on how to think and behave. Considering this potential, this project used Berger and Luckmann's (1967) Social Construction of Reality to help assess the potential meaning and power of the images of Black women in reality television docusoaps. According to social constructionists, individuals use information from social institutions (such as mass media) to help them construct their ideas about the real world. Although media images are not the only source of information for viewers, they are used in connection with other sources (Baran & Davis, 2009; Berger & Luckmann, 1967).

Researchers have also used the Social Construction of Reality to help illustrate how reality television constructs ideas about topics such as fatherhood (Smith, 2008) and female relationships (Chittenden, 2011). This theory was used in this project to help determine what images of Black women were constructed in reality television docusoaps and the way in which this constructed reality could impact audiences' construction of reality. While analyzing these images, research on images of Black women was also analyzed to see if stereotypical images continued to exist in docusoaps. The way in which each group was constructed and presented was compared to determine if Black women were presented more favorably depending on the racial make-up of the cast.

According to Berger and Luckmann (1967), individuals construct reality through their interaction and communication with each other. Roles and behaviors that become habitual are turned into patterns. These patterns become a part of individuals' realities. According to the theory, people are first born into an objective world with an objective reality that "has a history that antedates the individual's birth and is not accessible to his biographical recollection" (Berger & Luckmann, 1967, p. 60). As individuals grow up, they go through two levels of socialization. During the first level, primary socialization, a person becomes a part of society. It is through interactions with others that individuals begin to make sense of different roles and to create their own identity. Individuals also attempt to understand (Berger & Luckmann, 1967) how others make sense of the world in order to help themselves to do the same.

Berger and Luckmann (1967) explained that primary socialization serves as the basis for secondary socialization. According to Social Construction of Reality,

> ...primary socialization ends when the concept of the generalized other (and all that goes with it) has been established in the consciousness of the individual. At this point [he or she] is an effective member of society and in subjective possession of self and the world (Berger & Luckmann, 1967, p. 137).

Thus, at this point, the individual begins to have a more subjective understanding of the world based on interactions and communication with others. However, socialization does not stop at this point. The construction of reality and identity is continuous (Baran & Davis, 2009; Berger & Luckmann, 1967).

This ongoing construction of reality leads to secondary socialization during which individuals create and internalize realities about their different subworlds (i.e., different subgroups, subcultures, or subpopulations). In some instances during secondary socialization, new information can conflict with information that was internalized during primary socialization (Berger & Luckmann, 1967). For example a young Black woman's socialization as a member of the millennial generation (e.g., through interaction with peers) may conflict with what she learned about herself and her surroundings during primary socialization (e.g., what she was taught by her parents).

Baran and Davis (2009) discussed how different institutions help individuals continuously construct reality. The researchers explained that, "According to social constructionists, social institutions wield enormous power over culture because we as individuals view the culture they propagate as having a reality beyond our control" (p. 309). An example of such an institution is mass media. Media create meaning that is "socially constructed but has less input from audiences members and is beyond their control" (Baran & Davis, 2009, p. 309). Gamson, Croteau, Hoynes, and Sasson (1992) made a similar argument:

> We walk around with media-generated images of the world, using them to construct meaning about political and social issues. The lens through which we receive these images is not neutral but evinces the power and point of view of the political and economic elites who operate and focus it. (p. 374)

Researchers have found that television images help audience members construct reality as the Social Construction of Reality posits. For example, Peterson and Peters (1983) found that adolescents use television images, combined with their interactions with their peers, in order to construct meaning and reality. We sought to explore this relationship between television images and the way that viewers might construct meaning and reality. More specifically, this book project undertook the task of investigating how reality television—a type of programming that promises to give audience members more control—can construct reality about Black women.

We began this project by analyzing six docusoaps that aired during the 2011 season. We wanted to see how Black women within the six docusoaps (three in which Blacks were the numerical majority and three in which Black characters were the numerical minority) were presented, and we wanted to see in what ways, if any, their presentation resembled and differed from past images of Black women. The images were not solely stereotypical. For example, Black women were presented as being physically attractive (in ways outside of Eurocentric standards), were shown in healthy relationships with other women, were not always presented as hypersexual animals, and were featured as members of the upper class. Some could use this as an argument for how the images of Black women are improving. However, overall, the number of unflattering images across all of the docusoaps outweighed the number of flattering images.

Positive portrayals such as the Professional Black Woman and the Good Black Mother were only presented within the shows in which Blacks were in the numerical majority. Such positive depictions were discussed more within the cast biographies than within the shows' storylines.

One might speculate that the reason the shows with a numerical Black majority showed the more positive images of the Black women could be due to the "target audience" of these shows. For example, E. Franklin Frazier (1957/1997) talked about the importance of the performance of Black identity in his groundbreaking book, *Black Bourgeoisie*. Applying one facet of Frazier's argument, one might propose that these predominantly Black shows could appeal to Black audiences and Black audiences' desire for the ascription of success and affluence. Thus, shows might show Blacks living affluent lifestyles, in successful careers, etc. The difference between the actual Black bourgeoisie and what we might see on reality television is that the actual Black bourgeoisie performed their identity and class status as the upper elite whereas in these docusoaps viewers see Black affluence but without Blacks performing the "pretense" usually stereotypically associated with the upper class. For example, in Frazier's work Blacks created debutante balls to introduce young Black children to society, just as European aristocrats would and continue to host extravagant balls. A key finding from Frazier's work was that it was important for Blacks to demonstrate their upper-class status both in material possessions as well as in their conduct in public. However, what we see in many of these docusoaps is just one half of the bourgeoisie equation. Blacks demonstrate upper-class status by the material possessions; however, the behaviors such as fighting in public, drinking, gambling, and public promiscuity for example are not the behaviors associated with the erudite, refined, urbane, sophisticated, Black bourgeoisie (Waymer, 2011).

On the other hand, in several other reality television subgenres (Andrejevic & Coby, 2006; Boylorn, 2008; Pozner, 2010; Tyree, 2011), the negative portrayal of Black women as mean, aggressive, angry, and bitchy was featured across the majority of the docusoaps in our 2011 analysis. As researchers have argued, the improvement in media representations (that is the increase in numerical presentation) has not eliminated the stereotypical images of Black women (hooks, 1992; Nelson, 1998; Croteau & Hoynes, 2003; Glascock, 2003; Gray, 2004).

To state the initial findings succinctly, more flattering images of Black women were featured within the shows with a predominantly Black cast, whereas the majority of unflattering images of Black women were mostly found within the docusoaps in which the Black women were the minority. Within these shows where Black women constituted the minority, the image of the sexualized Black woman was common—to be found in other subgenres of reality television (Campbell et al., 2008; Pozner, 2010). In shows such as the *Real World,* a successful Black woman might not fit the dynamic that producers are trying to create on the show; thus, they might cast a particular "type" of Black woman for better ratings. A key question is whether this trope of the sexualized, aggressive Black woman is what the audiences expect and/or desire or whether producers are relying on such tropes because the tropes have been a part of the cultural landscape for years, are easily assessable by viewers since they are part of some viewers' mental schemas, and thus make for compelling yet predictable narratives.

Regardless of the answer to that question, the presence of the sexualized Black woman (in those shows which Black women were in the numerical minority) and the presence of the mean Black woman (in both sets of shows) were the two major similarities between research on reality television and the docusoaps we analyzed. In addition, the importance of beauty and femininity was still stressed. Within the shows where Black women were the numerical minority, Eurocentric beauty standards were still important. The presentations within the docusoaps were different from research on other subgenres of reality in that the lack of domesticity depicted was not treated as a failure for the majority of the women, as it was in lifestyle docusoaps (Fairclough, 2004). Instead, the women were discussed in their biographies as being good mothers who had careers. Women were also featured exhibiting anger more often than sadness, which was not the case in reality television dating shows (Dubrofsky, 2011). Again, we wonder what role the target audience plays in how Black women are cast and how they perform Black femininity on these shows.

Berger and Luckmann's (1967) Social Construction of Reality helps explain the potential implications of these findings. Based on this theory, information from social institutions, such as mass media, is used by individuals in order to construct ideas about the real world. To apply this theory to this book, audience members may adopt recurring characters and messages from these docusoaps as they construct ideas about everyday Black women. Dominant presentations of Black women may lead audiences to view Black women outside of the shows in the same way. Such a construction of reality could, in turn, impact attitudes toward this group and self-concepts among members of this group.

Bell-Jordan (2008) argued that reality television made a promise to address race relations but failed to do so within the storylines. Research on reality television also discusses the potential that this subgenre has to promote diversity and to impact race relations (Andrejevic, 2004; Andrejevic & Colby, 2006; Ouellette & Murray, 2009; Pozner, 2010; Pullen, 2004). Despite the presence of race in the docusoaps, racial issues and stereotypes were not discussed in the storylines. In this sense, reality television failed to meet its potential for creating diversity.

Dubrofsky (2011) found that Whiteness was privileged in reality dating shows as Black women were irrelevant in the general storyline. Her argument is also supported by some of the findings from the docusoaps in which Black women were the numerical minority. As discussed earlier, the Black cast members in *Khloe & Lamar* and *The Real World: Cancun* often had only small speaking roles. Their screen time appeared to increase as they exhibited more outrageous behavior. For example, in *The Real World: Cancun*, Jasmine was featured more when she was behaving like the Mean Black Woman, and Jonna appeared more when she was behaving like the sexualized Black woman. In other instances, the women were in the background or as part of group conversations but with small speaking roles. The women in *The Bad Girls Club: New Orleans* were featured more often but were also shown behaving more like mean, sexualized Black women.

Furthermore, several elements within the shows supported the idea that the Black women took part in their own oppression, as argued by Campbell et al. (2008). The shamelessness attached to mean Black women and the sexualized Black woman helped illustrate how the women accepted these labels. Critics argue that editing processes of reality television prevent true representations of its participants (Palmer, 2002; Pullen, 2004). However, all audiences may not view these images as false presentations because the actions are glamorized by the participants and portrayed as their own choices. Furthermore, the cast biographies of the shows where Black women were in the numerical majority framed the women in a positive and flattering light. When these images are not upheld in the presentations, that is, when the images are inconsistent with the biographical narratives, viewers may assume this to mean that the women's own actions present them in a negative fashion—not the show's creators.

The second part of this study analyzed docusoaps that aired in 2014 in which Black women were leading characters and/or in the numerical majority. This was done for one primary reason: In light of recent calls for greater accountability (boycotts of some reality TV programming) in the presentation of Black women in reality television, we wanted to see if the positive images we found in the analysis of 2011 shows persisted for Black women in 2014. What we found most telling was that the majority of the images have the potential to yield more positive reading from audiences. Each of the emergent themes is discussed below.

Black women were depicted as *reclaiming sexuality*. In the majority of cases, women were not depicted as hypersexualized, but rather as having healthy sexual relations, engaging in thoughtful and reflective discussions about their sexuality. Although the women still did not attach shame to their behaviors (as was the case in the 2011 episodes), the context of their discussions and actions may lead to a more favorable reading. For example, sex was often discussed in reference to committed relationships and was not villainized by others on the show. In terms of *physical appearance*, Black women were shown as defining beauty broadly and embodying a full range of what constitutes beauty. They did not adhere to strict Eurocentric standards of what constituted beauty; rather, they sometimes wore short, natural hair styles or long, woven hair extensions, embraced darker skin as beautiful or celebrated lighter skin as beautiful, and embraced different body types as beautiful. *Black motherhood* was a theme that was prevalent and portrayed in a positive light. The women took motherhood seriously, cared deeply for their children, sacrificed for their children, and found ways—albeit sometimes difficult ways—to balance career and motherhood. Financial and social independence from husbands, partners, and significant others was a major theme that emerged in the analysis of these docusoaps. "She Has Her Own (Money)" is how we categorized this theme in one chapter. It was important for the women—even when married to wealthy doctors or professional athletes—to have their own businesses, own careers, charities they were involved with, and their own identities. The women provided solid examples that challenged dominant notions of domesticity. Even on shows such as *Basketball Wives*, which posits them as affiliated with successful professional athletes—these women argue the importance of independence in this context. The final (negative) theme, "Girl Fight," depicts the women as confrontational at times, and loud and angry at times. Verbal and at times physical confrontations emerged during these shows. Although this theme is primarily the only negative theme that emerged, its implications of this theme further exacerbate the problems of mediated depictions in general and Black women's mediated depictions in docusoaps specifically.

Research in marketing, public relations, and management communication shows that a consumer is likely to be more vocal about a negative experience than a positive experience. Thus, this finding might provide a context and rationale for much of the negative attention that these docusoaps receive—especially in the context of viewers calling for boycotts of this programming. In short, people remember the negative more than the positive (especially in the areas of advertising and PR), so even though the images of Black women in docusoaps are mostly positive, the audience reaction would suggest otherwise (with boycotts and other protests).

This has serious implications because it appears the increased number of positive images might not be enough to overshadow the negatives. Is there any amount of positive imagery that can overshadow the negative imagery? Or is it more difficult to focus on positive images when the negative images have been so longstanding and have such strong historical underpinnings? Must reality television docusoaps featuring Black women be devoid of all negative imagery if they are to be free from boycotts, criticism, and audience outrage? Or would viewers be content with realistically flawed characters if such a heavy focus weren't placed on such stereotypical characters as the angry Black woman?

What we know is that drama sells. And if this is the most memorable message that producers and cast members internalize, then no amount of positive imagery might be able to overcome those negative images ...at least in the eyes of the most vocal critics of Black women's media depictions in docusoaps. Boylorn (2008) argues that outrageous behavior earns Black women more camera time. For this reason, sadly, the presence of the aggressive, angry, and Sapphire-like character may never disappear. And, because drama is so profitable for producers, advertisements and commercials are more likely to sensationalize the image of the angry Black women rather than focus on the several more flattering images, found within our analysis.

Thus, a major contribution of this book is the finding that despite the popular press and blogs and such, docusoap programming in which Black women are represented in a numerical majority or at least two Black women have leading roles, depicts predominantly more positive images of Black women than negative ones. Again, this seems to challenge conventional wisdom. This exploratory study then allows us to pose larger societal questions as well as a larger question about this subgenre of reality television: The question is not about the quantity of positive versus negative images but rather the question is about what constitutes the most memorable messages?

It is important to note that we do not attribute these images of Black women in docusoaps solely to participants and their desires, nor do we attribute all characterization to producers' editorial decisions. Instead, we illustrate how Black women are presented to the audience, regardless of who controls the actual images and/or dictates their behaviors. In several instances, the women's actions are *presented* as their own choice. Scholars (Biressi & Nunn, 2005; Couldry, 2009) make a good argument that viewers must understand how production teams and the presence of cameras influence cast members' behaviors. Research has also shown that audiences often consider both fictional and non-fictional televised images to be reflections of society in some way (Biressi & Nunn, 2005; Croteau & Hoynes, 2003; Gandy, 1998; Pozner, 2010). Thus, regardless of whether audience members understand these presentations as being true reflections of the Black women or of the production teams' decisions, there is still a potential influence by and from these mediated images. These images of Black women can still be used by viewers to construct their opinions of and about real Black women. We acknowledge that viewers are active audience members and the docusoap presentations are open to interpretation. While some may view reality television portrayals to be entirely derogatory, we found that several images of the women do have the potential for a more positive reading. This is even in the midst of the longstanding theme of the angry, aggressive Black woman. We just hope that viewers give the positive images more credence than the negative ones.

REFERENCES

Abraham, L. (2003). Media stereotypes of African Americans. In P. M. Lester & S. D. Ross (Eds.) *Images that injure: Pictorial stereotypes in the media* (pp. 87–92). Westport, CT: Praeger Publishers.

AMC Networks (2014). Premiere of WEtv's *Marriage Boot Camp*: Reality stars deliver more than 1.3 million total viewers. Retrieved from http://www.amcnetworks.com/press-releases/premiere-of-we-tvs-marriage-boot-camp-reality-stars-deliver-more-than-1-3-million-total-viewers

Andrejevic, M. (2004). *Reality TV: The work of being watched*. Lanham, MD: Rowman & Littlefield.

Andrejevic, M. & Colby, D. (2006). Racism and reality TV: The case of MTV's *Road Rules*. In D. S. Escoffery (Ed.) *How real is reality TV?: Essays on representation and truth* (pp. 195–211). Jefferson, NC: McFarland & Company.

Banet-Weiser, S., & Portwood-Stacer, L. (2006). I just want to be me again!: Beauty pageants, reality television, and post-feminism. *Feminist Theory, 7*, 255–272.

Baran, S. J. & Davis, D. K. (2009). *Mass communication theory: Foundations, ferment, and future*, (5th ed.) Boston, MA: Wadsworth Cengage Learning.

Barnes-Thomas, C. (2010, April 28). The mess reality TV is making of Black women: While some only have themselves to blame for the stereotypes, we all suffer. *The Loop*. Retrieved from http://www.theloop21.com/news/rant-reality-tv

Bell-Jordan, K. E. (2008). Black, White, and a survivor of *The Real World*: Constructions of race on reality TV. *Critical Studies of Media Communication, 25*(2), 353–372.

Berger, P. L. & T. Luckmann. (1967). *The social construction of reality: A treatise in the sociology of knowledge*. Garden City, NY: Anchor Books.

Berry, B. (2007). *Beauty bias: Discrimination and social power*. Westport, CT: Praeger.

Biressi, A. & Nunn, H. (2005). *Reality TV: Realism and revelation*. London: Wallflower.

Bitchie, N. & Kimmy. (2011, November 9). Kandi defends negative portrayals of black women on reality TV. Necole Bitchie. Retrieved from http://necolebitchie.com/2011/11/09/kandi-talks-negative-portrayals-of-black-women-on-reality-tv/

Black, E. (2012, May 14). Tami Roman offers Kesha Nichols a public apology. Retrieved from http://blog.vh1.com/2012-05-14/tami-roman-offers-kesha-nichols-a-public-apology/

Black, E. (2014, May 7). 5.6 million viewers tuned in to *Love & Hip Hop Atlanta*, Season 3 premiere. Retrieved from http://blog.vh1.com/2014–05-07/love-hip-hop-atlanta-season-3-ratings/

Boylorn, R. M. (2008). As seen on TV: An autoethnographic reflection on race and reality television. *Critical Studies of Media Communication*, 25(4), 413–433.

BravoMedia (2014). Bravo earns most-watched second quarter in its history. Retrieved from http://corporate.comcast.com/news-information/news-feed/bravo-earns-most-watched-second-quarter-in-history

BravoTV. (2011). *The Real Housewives of Atlanta*. Retrieved from http://www.bravotv.com/the-real-housewives-of-atlanta

Bruzzi, S. (2000). *New documentary: A critical introduction*. New York: Routledge.

Byerly, C. M. (2007). Situating "the other": Women, racial, and sexual minorities in the media. In P. J. Creedon & J. Cramer (Eds.), *Women in mass communication*, 3rd edition (pp. 221–232). Thousand Oaks, CA: Sage.

Campbell, S. D., Giannini, S. S., China, C. R., & Harris, C. S. (2008). I love New York: Does New York love me? *Journal of International Women's Studies*, 10(2), 20–28.

Caputi, J. (1999). The pornography of everyday life. In M. Meyers (Ed.), *Mediated women: Representations in popular culture* (pp. 57–80). Cresskill, NJ: Hampton Press.

Cavender, G., Bond-Maupin, L., & Jurik, N. C. (1999). The construction of gender in reality crime TV. *Gender & Society*, 13, 643–663.

Chittenden, T. (2011). Do you understand what you're accusing me of? Confrontational conversation in MTV's *The Hills* as a means of identity construction and social positioning in young female adults. *Popular Communication*, 9(3), 196–211.

Clissold, B. D. (2004). *Candid Camera* and the origins of reality TV: Contextualizing a historical precedent. In S. Holmes & D. Jermyn (Eds.), *Understanding reality television* (pp. 33–53). New York: Routledge.

Coleman, R. M. (2011). Roll up your sleeves: Black women, black feminism in "Feminist Media Studies." *Feminist Media Studies*, 11(1), 35–41.

Coleman, R. R. M. (2000). *African American viewers and the black situation comedy: Situating racial humor*. New York: Routledge.

Coleman, R. R. M. (2002). Introduction. In R. R. M. Coleman (Ed.), *Say it loud: African-American audiences, media, and identity* (pp. 1–26). New York: Routledge.

Coleman, R. R. M. (2003). Black sitcom portrayals. In G. Dines & J. M. Humez (Eds.), *Gender, race and class in media: A text-reader*, 2nd edition (pp. 79–88). Thousand Oaks, CA: Sage.

Collins, P. H. (1998). Mammies, matriarchs, and other controlling images. In E. C. Eze (Ed.) *African philosophy: An anthology* (pp. 346–354). Malden, MA: Blackwell.

Collins, P. H. (2005). *Black sexual politics*. New York: Routledge.

Collins, P. H. (2009). *Black feminist thought: Knowledge, consciousness, and the politics of empowerment* (2nd ed.). New York: Routledge.

Corner, J. (2009). Performing the real: Documentary diversions. In S. Murray & L. Ouellette (Eds.), *Reality TV: Remaking television culture*, 2nd edition (pp. 44–64). New York: New York University Press.

Couldry, N. (2009). Teaching us to fake it: The ritualized norms of television's reality games. In S. Murray & L. Ouellette (Eds.), *Reality TV: Remaking television culture*, 2nd edition (pp. 82–99). New York: New York University Press.

Cramer, J. & Creedon, P. J. (2007). Introduction: We've come a long way, maybe. In P. J. Creedon & J. Cramer (Eds.), *Women in mass communication*, 3rd edition (pp. 3–8). Thousand Oaks, CA: Sage.

Croteau, D. & Hoynes, W. (2003). *Media/society: Industries, images, and audiences* (3rd ed.). Thousand Oaks, CA: Pine Forge.

Danesi, M. (2008). *Popular culture: Introductory perspectives*. Lanham, MD: Rowman & Littlefield.

Douglas, S. J. (2010). *The rise of enlightened sexism: How pop culture took us from girl power to girls gone wild*. New York: St. Martin's.

Douglas, S. (2004). Young women learn harmful gender stereotypes from reality TV. In K. Balkin (Ed.), *Reality TV* (pp. 61–63). Farmington Hills, MI: Greenhaven.

Douglas, S. (1994). *Where the girls are: Growing up female with the mass media*. New York: Times Books.

Dubrofsky, R. E. (2009). Fallen women in reality TV: A pornography of emotion. *Feminist Media Studies*, 9(3), 353–368.

Dubrofsky, R. E. (2011). *The surveillance of women on reality television: Watching* The Bachelor *and the* Bachelorette. Lanham, MD: Lexington.

Dubrofsky, R. E. & Hardy, A. (2008). Performing race in *Flavor of Love* and *The Bachelor Critical Studies of Media Communication*, 25(2), 373–392.

Dunkley, C. (2002). It's not new and it's not clever. In D. Cummings (Ed.), *Reality TV: How real is real?* (pp. 35–46). Oxford: Hodder & Stoughton.

E! Online. (2011). *Khloe & Lamar*. Retrieved from http://www.eonline.com/on/shows/khloe_and_lamar/index.html

Edwards, L. H. (2004). What a girl wants: Gender norming in reality game shows. *Feminist Media Studies*, 4(2), 226–228.

Elliott, D. (2003). Moral responsibilities and the power of pictures. In P. M. Lester & S. D. Ross (Eds.), *Images that injure: Pictorial stereotypes in the media* (pp. 7–14). Westport, CT: Praeger.

Engstrom, E. (2009). Creation of a new "empowered" female identity in WEtv's *Bridezillas*. *Media Report to Women*, 37(1), 6–12.

Entman, R. & Rojecki, A. (2000). *The black image in the white mind*. Chicago: University of Chicago Press.

EURweb (2014, May 20). WE tv's 'Mary Mary' sees double digit growth in Season 3. Retrieved from http://www.eurweb.com/2014/05/we-tvs-mary-mary-sees-double-digit-growth-in-season-3/

Fairclough, K. (2004). Women's work? *Wife Swap* and the reality problem. *Feminist Media Studies*, 4(2), 344–347.

Frazier, E. F. (1997). *Black Bourgeoisie*. New York: Free Press Paperbacks.

Friedlander, W. (2014, March 20). WE TV renews *SWV Reunited*, *Braxton Family Values*. Retrieved from http://variety.com/2014/tv/news/we-tv-renews-swv-reunited-braxton-family-values-1201140402/

Friedman, J. (2002). Introduction. In J. Friedman (Ed.), *Reality squared: Televisual discourse on the real* (pp. 1–24). New Brunswick, NJ: Rutgers University Press.

Gamson, W. A., Croteau, D., Hoynes, W., & Sasson, T. (1992). Media images and the social construction of reality. *Annual Review of Sociology*, 18, 373–393.

Gauntlett, D. (2008). *Media, gender and identity: An introduction* (2nd ed.). New York: Routledge.

Gillan, J. (2004). From Ozzie Nelson to Ozzy Osbourne: The genesis and development of the reality (star) sitcom. In S. Holmes & D. Jermyn (Eds.), *Understanding reality television* (pp. 54–70). New York: Routledge.

Glascock, J. (2003). Gender, race, and aggression in newer TV networks' primetime programming. *Communication Quarterly*, 51, 90–101.

Goldman, A. & Waymer, D. (2014). Identifying ugliness, defining beauty: A focus group analysis of and reaction to *Ugly Betty*. *The Qualitative Report*, 19(20), 1–19. Retrieved from http://www.nova.edu/ssss/QR/QR19/waymer20.pdf

Gorman, B. (2011, April 12). Sunday cable ratings: "Army Wives," "The Killing" steady; "Breakout Kings" falls; Plus "Human Planet," "Khloe & Lamar," & much more. *TV by the Numbers*. Retrieved from http://tvbythenumbers.zap2it.com/2011/04/12/sunday-cable-ratings-the-killing-steady-breakout-kings-falls-plus-human-planet-khloe-lamar-much-more/89051/

Graham-Bertolini, A. (2004). *Joe Millionaire* as fairy tale: A feminist critique. *Feminist Media Studies*, 4(2), 341–343.

Gray, H. (2004). *Watching race: Television and the struggle for blackness*. Minneapolis: University of Minnesota Press.

Gray, J. (2008). Cinderella burps: Gender, performativity, and the dating show. In S. Murray & L. Ouellette (Eds.), *Reality TV: Remaking television culture*, 2nd edition (pp. 260–277). New York: New York University Press.

Haggins, B. (2001). Why Beulah and Andy still play today: Minstrelsy in the New Millennium. *Emergencies*, 11(2), 249–267.

Hall, S. (2003). The whites of their eyes: Racist ideologies and the media. In G. Dines & J. M. Humez (Eds.), *Gender, race, and class in media: A text-reader*, 2nd edition (pp. 89–93). Thousand Oaks, CA: Sage.

Harris-Perry, M. V. (2011). *Sister citizen: Shame, stereotypes, and Black women in America*. New Haven, CT: Yale University Press.

Hine, D. C. (1996). *Speak truth to power: Black professional class in United States history*. Brooklyn, NY: Carlson.

Ho, R. (2014). *Real Housewives of Atlanta* hits record ratings; Kim Zolciak open to returning. Retrieved from http://www.accessatlanta.com/weblogs/radio-tv-talk/2014/jan/07/real-housewives-atlanta-hits-record-ratings-sunday/

Holmes, S. (2004). All you've got to worry about is the task, having a cup of tea, and doing a bit of sunbathing: Approaching celebrity in *Big Brother*. In S. Holmes & D. Jermyn (Eds.), *Understanding reality television* (pp. 111–135). New York: Routledge.

Holmes, S. & Jermyn, D. (2004). Introduction: Understanding reality TV. In S. Holmes and D. Jermyn (Eds.), *Understanding reality television* (pp. 1–32). New York: Routledge.

Holtzman, L. & Sharpe, L. (2014). *Media messages: What film, television, and popular music teach us about race, class, gender, and sexual orientation*. Armonk, NY: M. E. Sharpe.

hooks, b. (1992). *Black looks: Race and representations*. Cambridge, MA: South End Press.

hooks, b. (2008). *Outlaw culture: Resisting representations*. New York: Routledge.

Hudson, S. V. (1998). Re-creational television: The paradox of change and continuity within stereotypical iconography. *Sociological Inquiry*, 68(2), 242–257.

Huff Post TV (2012, June 5). *Basketball Wives* Reunion: Instead of fighting, the women were apologizing to one another. Retrieved from http://www.huffingtonpost.com/2012/06/05/basketball-wives-reunion-women-apologizing-video_n_1569871.html

Jermyn, D. (2004). This is about real people! Video technologies, actuality and affect in the television crime appeal. In S. Holmes & D. Jermyn (Eds.), *Understanding Reality Television* (pp. 71–90). New York: Routledge.

Jewell, K. S. (1993). *From Mammy to Miss America and beyond: Cultural images & the shaping of US social policy*. New York: Routledge.

Johnston, E. (2006). How women really are: Disturbing parallels between reality television and 18th century fiction. In D. S. Escoffery (Ed.), *How real is reality TV? Essays on representation and truth* (pp. 115–132). Jefferson, NC: McFarland & Company.

Kelley, R. D. G. (1996). *Into the fire: African Americans since 1970*. New York: Oxford University Press.

Kilborn, R. (1994). How real can you get?: Recent developments in "reality" television. *European Journal of Communication*, 9, 421–439.

Kraszewski, J. (2009). Country hicks and urban cliques: Mediating race, reality, and liberalism on MTV's The Real World. In S. Murray & L. Ouellette (Eds.), *Reality TV: Remaking television culture*, 2nd edition (pp. 205–222). New York: New York University Press.

Linn, T. (2003). Media methods that lead to stereotypes. In P. M. Lester & S. D. Ross (Eds.), *Images that injure: Pictorial stereotypes in the media* (pp. 23–27). Westport, CT: Praeger.

Littlefield, M. B. (2008). The media as a system of racialization: Exploring images of African-American women and the new racism. *American Behavioral Scientist*, 51(5), 675–685.

Lucas, K. & D'Enbeau, S. (2013). Moving beyond themes: Reimagining the qualitative analysis curriculum. *Qualitative Communication Research*, 2, 213–227.

M., A. (2012). Don't support Evelyn Lozada's spinoff show *EV and OCHO* on VH1. Retrieved from https://www.change.org/p/boycott-basketball-wives-evelyn-lozada-don-t-support-evelyn-lozada-s-spinoff-show-ev-and-ocho-on-vh1

Macdonald, M. (1995). *Representing women: Myths of femininity in popular media.* New York: Edward Arnold.
Magder, T. (2009). Television 2.0: The business of American television in transition. In S. Murray & L. Ouellette (Eds.), *Reality TV: Remaking television culture*, 2nd edition (pp. 141–164). New York: New York University Press.
Mascaro, T. (2004). Shades of black on homicide: Advances and retreats in portrayals of African-American women. *The Journal of Popular Film and Television, 32,* 56–67.
Mazzarella, S. R. & Pecora, N. O. (1999). Introduction. In S. R. Mazzarella & N. O. Pecora (Eds.), *Growing up girls: Popular culture and the construction of identity* (pp. 1–8). New York: Peter Lang.
McElya, M. (2007). *Clinging to Mammy: The faithful slave in twentieth-century America.* Cambridge, MA: Harvard University Press.
Meyers, M. (1999). Fracturing women. In M. Meyers (Ed.), *Mediated women: Representations in popular culture* (pp. 3–24). Cresskill, NJ: Hampton.
Moorti, S. & Ross, K. (2004). Reality television: Fairy tale or feminist nightmare? *Feminist Media Studies,* 4(2), 203–205.
MTV. (2011). *The Real World San Diego.* Retrieved from http://www.mtv.com/shows/real_world/san_diego/series.jhtml
Murray, S. (2009). I think we need a new name for it: The meeting of documentary and reality TV. In S. Murray & L. Ouellette (Eds.) *Reality TV: Remaking television culture*, 2nd edition (pp. 65–81). New York: New York University Press.
NBC Universal (2014). Bravo media continues record ratings earning best quarter in network history. Retrieved from http://www.nbcuni.com/corporate/newsroom/bravo-media-continues-record-ratingsearning-best-quarter-in-network-history/
Nelson, A. M. (1998). Black situation comedies and the politics of television art. In Y. R. Kamlipour & T. Carilli (Eds.), *Cultural diversity and the US media* (pp. 79–87). Albany, NY: State University of New York Press.
Nordyke, K. (2011, February 2). *Real Housewives of Atlanta* wraps on record note. *Reuters.* Retrieved from http://in.reuters.com/article/2011/02/02/us-bravo-idINTRE7111IR201102
Ono, K. A. (2008). The biracial subject as passive receptacle for Japanese American memory in *Come See the Paradise.* In M. Beltran & C. Fojas (Eds.) *Mixed race Hollywood* (pp. 136–156). New York: New York University Press.
Ouellette, L. & Hay, J. (2008). *Better living through reality TV.* Malden, MA: Blackwell.
Ouellette, L. & Murray, S. (2009). Introduction. In S. Murray & L. Ouellette (Eds.) *Reality TV: Remaking television culture*, 2nd edition (pp. 1–19). New York: New York University Press.
Oxygen. (2011). *The Bad Girls Club: New Orleans.* Retrieved from http://bad-girls-club.oxygen.com/
Palmer, G. (2002). *Big Brother*: An experiment in governance. *Television and New Media* 3(3), 295–310.
Perry, L. (2003). Who(se) am I?: The identity and image of women in hip-hop. In G. Dines & J. M. Humez (Eds.), *Gender, race, and class in media: A Text-reader*, 2nd edition (pp. 136–147). Thousand Oaks, CA: Sage.

Peterson, G. W. & Peters, D. F. (1983). Adolescents' construction of social reality. *Youth & Society, 15*(1), 67.

Popular Critic. (2012, March 1). Star Jones supports *Basketball Wives* boycott with Wendy Williams. *Atlanta Black Star*. Retrieved from http://atlantablackstar.com/2012/03/01/star-jones-supports-basketball-wives-boycott-with-wendy-williams/

Pozner, J. L. (2010). *Reality bites back: The troubling truth about guilty pleasure TV*. Berkeley, CA: Seal.

Pullen, C. (2004). The household, the basement and *The Real World*: Gay identity in the constructed reality environment. In S. Holmes & D. Jermyn (Eds.), *Understanding Reality Television* (pp. 211–232). New York: Routledge.

Raphael, C. (2009). The political economic origins of reality TV. In S. Murray & L. Ouellette (Eds.), *Reality TV: Remaking television culture*, 2nd edition (pp. 123–139). New York: New York University Press.

Reid, J. (2011, March 3). Fight night: Black women on reality TV. *The Root*. Retrieved from http://www.theroot.com/print/50566

Reid-Brinkley, S. R. (2008). The essence of res(ex)pectability: Black women's negotiation of black femininity in rap music and music video. *Meridians: Feminism, Race, Transnationalism, 8*(1), 236–260.

Rogers, D. D. (2003). Daze of our lives: The soap opera as feminine text. In G. Dines & J. M. Humez (Eds.), *Gender, race, and class in media: A text-reader*, 2nd edition (pp. 476–481). Thousand Oaks, CA: Sage.

Rowe, K. (1995). *The unruly woman: Gender and the genres of laughter*. Austin, TX: University of Texas Press.

Samuels, A. (2011, May 1). Reality TV trashes black women: An unsettling new formula—eye-rolling, finger-snapping stereotypes. *Newsweek Magazine*. Retrieved from http://www.thedailybeast.com/newsweek/2011/05/01/reality-tv-trashes-black-women.html

Schroeder, E. R. (2006). Sexual racism and reality television: Privileging the white male prerogative on MTV's *The Real World*. In D. S. Escoffery (Ed.), *How real is reality TV? Essays on representation and truth* (pp. 180–194). Jefferson, NC: McFarland & Company.

Scott, T. L. (2012, April 25). Star Jones forming anti-"BBW" coalition. *Sister2Sister Magazine*. Retrieved from http://s2smagazine.com/2012/04/25/star-jones-forming-anti-bbw-coalition/

Seidman, R. (2009, August 27). MTV *Real World: Cancun* #1 w/P12–34 nine weeks in a row. *TV by the Numbers*. Retrieved from http://tvbythenumbers.zap2it.com/2009/08/27/mtvs-real-world-cancun-1-wp12-34-nine-weeks-in-a-row/25551/

Seidman, R. (2011, August 16). Oxygen's *Hair Battle Spectacular* averages 874,000 viewers in season premiere. *TV by the Numbers*. Retrieved from http://tvbythenumbers.zap2it.com/2011/08/16/oxygens-hair-battle-spectacular-averages-averages-874000-viewers-in-season-2-premiere/100634/

Smith, D. C. (2008). Critiquing reality-based televisual black fatherhood; A critical analysis of Run's House and Snoop Dogg's Fatherhood. *Critical Studies of Media Communication, 25*(2), 393–412.

Smith-Shomade, B. E. (2002). *Shaded lives: African-American women and television*. Piscataway, NJ: Rutgers University Press.

Speight, S. L., Thomas, A. J. & Witherspoon, K. C. (2004). Toward the development of the stereotypic roles of Black women scale. *Journal of Black Psychology, 30*, 426–441.

Stephens, D. P. & Phillips, L. D. (2003). Freaks, gold diggers, divas, and dykes: The sociohistorical development of adolescent African-American women's sexual scripts. *Sexuality & Culture, Winter,* 3–47.

Stephens, R. L. (2004). Socially soothing stories? Gender, race and class in TLC's A Wedding Story and A Baby Story. In S. Holmes & D. Jermyn (Eds.), *Understanding reality television* (pp. 191–210). New York: Routledge.

Stern, D. (2005). MTV, reality television and the commodification of female sexuality in *The Real World*. *Media Report to Women, 33*(2), 13–21.

TV by the Numbers. (2014). VH1 primetime ratings rise 16% in adult 18–49 demographic in the second quarter of 2014. Retrieved from http://tvbythenumbers.zap2it.com/2014/06/30/vh1-primetime-ratings-rise-16-in-adult-18-49-demographic-in-the-second-quarter-of-2014/278180/

Tyree, T. (2009). Lovin' Momma and hatin' on Baby Mama: A comparison of misogynistic and stereotypical representations in songs about rappers' mothers and baby mamas. *Women and Language, 32*(2), 50–58.

Tyree, T. (2011). African American stereotypes in reality television. *The Howard Journal of Communications, 22,* 394–413.

Valdivia, A. N. (2005). Geographies of Latinidad: Deployments of radical hybridity in the mainstream. In C. McCarthy, W. Crichlow, and G. Dimitriadis (Eds.), *Race, identity, and representation in education* (pp. 307–320). New York: Routledge.

Vargas, Y. V. (2008). Marco said I look like charcoal: A Puerto Rican's exploration of her ethnic identity. *Qualitative Inquiry, 14,* 949–954.

Vasquez, L. (2010). Personal essay: Yo soy boricua. Retrieved from http://www.latina.com/entertainment/celebrity/personal-essay-yo-soy-boricua

Vh-1. (2011a). *Basketball Wives*. Retrieved from http://www.vh1.com/shows/basketball_wives/season_3/series.jhtml

Vh-1. (2011b). *Love & Hip Hop*. Retrieved from http://www.vh1.com/shows/love_and_hip_hop/series.jhtml

Viera, B. (2011, March 21). Are black women on reality TV a reflection of real life? *Clutch Magazine*. Retrieved from http://clutchmagonline.com/2011/03/are-black-women-on-reality-tv-a-reflection-of-real-life/

Waggoner, C. E. (2004). Reality disciplining female sexuality in *Survivor*. *Feminist Media Studies, 4*(2), 217–220.

Walsh-Childers, K. (2003). Women as sex partners. In P. M. Lester & S. D. Ross (Eds.), *Images that injure: Pictorial stereotypes in the media* (pp. 141–148). Westport, CT: Praeger.

Waymer, D. (2011). Hip-hop and capitalistic interests. In V. A. Young & B. H. Tsemo (Eds.), *From bourgeois to boojie: Black middle-class performances* (pp. 159–174). Detroit: Wayne State University Press.

We Tell All. (2013). *Marriage Boot Camp* renewed for Season 2. Retrieved from http://www.wetv.com/we-tell-all/blogs/marriage-boot-camp-renewed-for-season-2

West, C. M. (1995). Mammy, Sapphire, and Jezebel: Historical images of black women and their implications for psychotherapy. *Psychotherapy, 32*(3), 458–466.

WE tv, (2013, September 9). *L.A. Hair* is coming back for Season 3. Retrieved from http://www.wetv.com/we-tell-all/blogs/l-a-hair-is-coming-back-for-season-3

White, D. G. (1999). *Ar'n't I a woman? Female slaves in the plantation south.* New York: W. W. Norton & Company.

Williams, P. (2011, May 27). VH1 announces *Love & Hip Hop* Season 2, 10 more episodes to air. *Fresh Like Dougie.* Retrieved from http://freshlikedougie.com/celebrities/vh1-announces-love-and-hip-hop-season-2-10-more-episodes-to-air/

Wilson II, C. C., Guiterrez, F., & Chao, L. M. (2003). *Racism, sexism, and the media: The rise of class communication in multicultural America* (3rd ed.). Thousand Oaks, CA: Sage.

Witherspoon, C. (2014). *Blood, Sweat and Heels* star Mica Hughes: "I was told I'm too beautiful to be black". Retrieved from http://thegrio.com/2014/02/07/blood-sweat-and-heels-star-mica-hughes-i-was-told-im-too-beautiful-to-be-black/#54296363

YBF. (2013). *Basketball Wives* stars Tami, Evelyn and Shaunie dish to *Upscale* on weight issues, domestic abuse & backlash, reveal why Jennifer & Royce are "non-motherf***ing factors." Retrieved from http://theybf.com/2013/06/10/basketball-wives-stars-tami-evelyn-and-shaunie-dish-to-upscale-on-weight-issues-domestic

YBF. (2014). Activist group challenges Bravo—Stop profiting from Black women fighting! Retrieved from http://theybf.com/2014/11/10/activist-group-challenges-bravo-stop-profiting-from-black-women-fighting

Zook, K. B. (2010, May 24). Has reality TV become black women's enemy? The Root. Retrieved from http://www.theroot.com/views/has-realoty-tv-become-black-women-s-enemy

ROCHELLE BROCK &
RICHARD GREGGORY JOHNSON III,
Executive Editors

Black Studies and Critical Thinking is an interdisciplinary series which examines the intellectual traditions of and cultural contributions made by people of African descent throughout the world. Whether it is in literature, art, music, science, or academics, these contributions are vast and far-reaching. As we work to stretch the boundaries of knowledge and understanding of issues critical to the Black experience, this series offers a unique opportunity to study the social, economic, and political forces that have shaped the historic experience of Black America, and that continue to determine our future. Black Studies and Critical Thinking is positioned at the forefront of research on the Black experience, and is the source for dynamic, innovative, and creative exploration of the most vital issues facing African Americans. The series invites contributions from all disciplines but is specially suited for cultural studies, anthropology, history, sociology, literature, art, and music.

Subjects of interest include (but are not limited to):

- EDUCATION
- SOCIOLOGY
- HISTORY
- MEDIA/COMMUNICATION
- RELIGION/THEOLOGY
- WOMEN'S STUDIES
- POLICY STUDIES
- ADVERTISING
- AFRICAN AMERICAN STUDIES
- POLITICAL SCIENCE
- LGBT STUDIES

For additional information about this series or for the submission of manuscripts, please contact Dr. Brock (Indiana University Northwest) at brock2@iun.edu or Dr. Johnson (University of San Francisco) at rgjohnsoniii@usfca.edu.

To order other books in this series, please contact our Customer Service Department:

(800) 770-LANG (within the U.S.)
(212) 647-7706 (outside the U.S.)
(212) 647-7707 FAX

Or browse online by series at www.peterlang.com.

www.ingramcontent.com/pod-product-compliance
Ingram Content Group UK Ltd.
Pitfield, Milton Keynes, MK11 3LW, UK
UKHW021849210426
5322IPUK00022B/558